NEW COWBOY POETRY

NEW COWBOY POETRY

A CONTEMPORARY GATHERING

Edited and with an introduction by
Hal Cannon

PEREGRINE SMITH BOOKS

94 93 92   10 9 8 7 6

This is a Peregrine Smith Book, published
by Gibbs Smith, Publisher, P.O. Box 667,
Layton, Utah 84041

Design by J. Scott Knudsen

Cover illustration © Howard Post

Manufactured in the United States of
America

**LIBRARY OF CONGRESS
CATALOGING-IN-PUBLICATION DATA**

New cowboy poetry : a contemporary
gathering / edited by Hal Cannon.
          p.   cm.
  ISBN 0-87905-243-0
  1. Cowboys—Poetry. 2. Ranch life—
Poetry. 3. West (U.S.)—Poetry. 4. American
poetry—West (U.S.) 5. American poetry—20th
century.   I. Cannon, Hal, 1948—
PS595.C6N4   1990
811'.54080352636—dc90   89-26581
                                         CIP

The paper used in this publication meets the
minimum requirements of American National
Standard for Information Sciences—
Permanence of Paper for Printed Library
Materials, ANSI Z39.48-1984 ∞

CONTENTS

INTRODUCTION

When I read these poems I hear the voices of the poets and I see the places where the poems belong—the cowcamps, the cook houses, pickup trucks, small western-town bars. I hear Waddie Mitchell working out a poem as we drive across the loneliest highway in Nevada. I've been with Joel Nelson in the dark backstage at the Cowboy Poetry Gathering as tension takes over and he rapidly practices his poem over and over before going out front. I hear the voices that I know so well in the cowcamps as buckaroos sit around the fire, exhausted from a day of gathering cattle.

That's what makes the task of selecting so difficult—the voices, discarding hundreds of poems, and the poets who wrote them, for the few that are chosen for this book.

The voice is the essential part of the poem—it's the music. Beyond the written word is the creak of saddle leather, the deafening roar of the Yellowstone River, the sound of the most profound silence in the world—desert at midday. On a ranch in open country at night, you can hear all kinds of voices, animals, moving water, and air. Somewhere in those dark miles is the music of cowboy poetry.

The music is not just a spontaneous exultation of this lifestyle; it is a stabilizing tradition that has been with ranch people for over a century. Cowboy poetry is a folk art in every sense of the word. Folk art of the past, like all archaeological records, reflects ways of life and values far beyond the art itself. In judging folk art, it is the cultural group which retains the best of its art and discards the rest. Cowboy poetry is most appropriately judged, then, by cowboys; the most meaningful is memorized, recited, and passed down over time. The oldest of cowboy poetry—that which talks about cattle drives of the nineteenth century—is still alive in cow camps around the West. Even though cowboys today haven't experienced long and dangerous drives for six months at a time, they still sing and recite the verses that talk of a yearning for loved ones, a dread at not coming home alive. They aren't steeped in Victorian sentimentality that was part of the popular culture of that day; nevertheless, these poems and songs have meaning for them.

As the century turned, the cowboy way of life changed. The West was no longer an unpeopled, unfenced land; the long cattle drives ended and the ability for independence on the frontier was diminished. The cowboys felt these changes more acutely than most. Cowboys such as Curley Fletcher began celebrating the sport of cowboying by staging some of the earliest public rodeos and distributing poetry at these events. Bruce Kiskaddon, frustrated by the changing nature of his occupation, quit the ranch in 1925 and spent the rest of his life reminiscing through poetry the life loved and gone.

Simultaneously, unnumbered outsiders to the world of cows and horses began to capitalize on the cowboy as a myth figure. The visual surroundings of the occupation as depicted in art, the stories told in dime-store novels, the whole image of cowboy life as shown in movies and television, and the sound of cowboys in song reached a worldwide audience. Progressively, this popular image drifted away from reality. Even the insiders became more self-conscious of their role in the American romantic myth.

As the popular image drifted further away from the original, cowboy poetry became a stronger expression of the occupation from within. The cowboy ballads of the mid-twentieth century never punctured the consciousness of people outside the ranching occupation. Thus having little popular appeal, the poetry as performance existed only in cowcamps, and a published record of this folk art came out in trade magazines, local newspapers, and self-published books.

This brings us to the new resurgence of cowboy poetry's popularity which has taken place since 1985.

Wallace Stegner, in *A Sense of Place*, says that a place is not a place until a poet has been there. It has taken generations living in the West for its folk poetry to proclaim love of the land. People came to the West with a dream that rarely matched the harsh reality of living in the arid region. Though the pioneers survived, it took generations of family and friends buried in the local graveyards, trees growing up around the houses, irrigation making oases in the deserts, and a hundred years of painted sunsets for people to write convincingly about belonging to the sweeping vastness that became their home.

Today's cowboy poetry expresses a strong sentiment for place that did not exist in the early verse. Next to the government, ranchers hold more land in the West than any other group; so they know only too well that our world is shrinking, that stewardship of the land has attendant responsibilities which go beyond our generation.

All cowboy poets live in the rural West. At the center of the tradition are the men who spend the majority of their time horseback, keeping track of grazing cattle and moving them to market. Many of today's poets are ranch housewives, feed salesmen, ranch owners, auctioneers, rodeo cowboys, dude wranglers, and people that hold down eight-hour workaday jobs but raise cattle on the side. And it is probable that some of the best poetry is tucked in a bedroll and will never reach the public.

Though cowboy poetry has traditionally been dominated by men, an increasing number of women are writing about the ranching life. Subjects range from a woman's unique tenderness with animals, to how the new woman's role works on the ranch, to the comic variety of daily chores. Many women poets chronicle what it means to "buy into" the dream of the cowboy life.

In several ways, new cowboy poetry has followed the trends of American literature. For one, some cowboy poets have experimented successfully with new forms, including free verse. Another similarity with literary trends is that today's poetry is much more personal than the old-time verse. As well, themes in new poetry reflect contemporary world issues: technology, economy, government, environmental concerns.

The most profound difference between the new poets and the old is the bent toward public performance. Cowboy poetry has become a common part of church socials, country fairs, school programs, and cattlemen's dinners. Attendant with this performance aspect is the stronger ratio of humorous poetry being written today. Particularly popular is the method of putting to verse old jokes and stories which have been passed around cowcamps, bars, hunting parties, an even TV talk shows. The advent of this public entertainment has emanated from the Cowboy Poetry Gathering, held each January in Elko, Nevada, and reenacted in scores of state and regional gatherings of cowboy poets. There are probably fifty cowboy poets who make at least part of their living performing poetry as after-dinner speakers and entertainers. A few have even given up much of the ranch life to go on the road. Over a hundred poets have produced cassettes, videotapes, and books to accompany their performances.

Everyone was startled by the public interest in cowboy poetry: nearly every major magazine in America has published articles about it; popular talk shows regularly feature cowboy poets; attendance at cowboy poetry gatherings increases steadily—and these aren't just ranch folks coming to hear each other's latest works. Besides rural westerners, the audiences for the new cowboy poetry include university professors, car-parts salesmen, housewives from suburbia, and young executives from office towers on the coast. The poetry which affects these people so deeply must speak to more universal issues than the documenting of an occupation. In fact, the poems are parables for shared values and emotions: the reluctant man in a modern world; growing old and watching generations pass; the ancestral knowledge of dark earth, the smell of birth, and pastoral serenity in the wilderness.

This poetry is utilitarian—heavy-duty, industrial strength poetry. It is meant to be read aloud and, even better, memorized and recited. It is best used in the natural world where there are starlit skies, the warmth of blazing fires, and sounds and sights of open expanse. This book is meant to be carried with you in the glove box of a pickup truck, the back pocket of a worn pair of pants, even a saddlebag. It is not made to take up space on a library shelf, squeezed between other unread volumes. Take it along; you never know when the opportunity will be just right. Nothing pleases more than to see copies of the book twice as thick as the original from continued page turning, with turned-down corners marking favorite poems, or the whole shape curved to match the owner's posterior.

Our civilization puts a premium on the ability of poetry to say our most noble thoughts, to chronicle our history. The life of a cowboy is conducive to writing poetry. Endless hours moving slowly to the rhythm of a horse's gait, the vantage of sitting horseback several feet off the ground, living day in and day outside in nature, having to rely on animal intelligence to be at the right place at the right time, living within a display tradition which sets you apart from others by costume and gear, and living a demanding moral code—all these are elements of a lifestyle fit for contemplation and expression. This is why cowboy poetry is part of our literary tradition, to be valued for generations to come.

Hal Cannon
Western Folklife Center
December 1989

ACKNOWLEDGMENTS

This book of poems could not have been compiled without trust, friendship, and the willingness of cowboys and cowgirls to give their poems to the world by allowing their work to be printed. Cowboy poets generally are not wealthy, but they continually invest in their work by publishing it and traveling long western distances to attend cowboy poetry gatherings. My hat is off to these men and women.

The organizing of the Cowboy Poetry Gathering in Elko, Nevada, the event that was a catalyst for the cowboy poetry revival, could not have succeeded without the folklorists of the West and the dedication of the people of Elko, in particular, Tara McCarty and Meg Glaser.

The literary tradition of cowboy poetry is a long-standing one. The Fife Archive at Utah State University has collected cowboy poetry and continually makes it accessible to the public and to scholars.

Gibbs M. Smith and his publishing company are celebrating twenty years of service to literature. He grasped the idea of publishing cowboy poetry when no other publisher would consider it. To him and his dedicated staff, particularly Madge Baird, for her help in editing this book, I am indebted.

Illustrations herein are by Fred Lambert from *Bygone Days of the Old West,* and by Lewis E. Wallis from a book of poems by Wade Lane entitled *Cowboy Meditation.*

THERE'S SOMETHIN' THAT
A COWBOY KNOWS

DARRELL ARNOLD

There's somethin' that a cowboy knows
That makes him ride the land—
His choice, a life that only he
And God can understand.

> He knows that every day he lives
> Could be his very last,
> And so he must live while he can—
> Live hard, live good, live fast.

There's somethin' that a cowboy knows
That poorer men will not—
Like ridin' circles all day in
A fast, ground-eatin' trot.

> He knows the wild, flying charge
> Across a rocky hill,
> Astride a thousand pounds of horse—
> The rush, the joy, the thrill.

There's somethin' that a cowboy knows,
A kinship with the wind
That causes him to live alone,
His horse his closest friend.

> He knows a feeling in his heart
> That makes it seem worthwhile
> To drift alone and thus forsake
> A woman's touch and smile.

There's somethin' that a cowboy knows,
A scent born on the air
Of sage, and sweat, and leather,
And of smoke and burnin' hair.

He knows the pain of choking dust
That burns his blinded eyes.
He knows to pray for blessed rain
From empty, cloudless skies.

There's somethin' that a cowboy knows
About the break of day
That drags him from his soogans
'Fore the stars have cleared away.

He knows the pledge of springtime
When new life is all around,
Like tiny, shiny, wobbly calves
A-dryin' on the ground.

There's somethin' that a cowboy knows
'Bout livin' 'neath the sky,
Out there where men have room to live
And also, room to die.

He knows the blast of winter storms
When cold cuts like a knife
Right through his coat and woollies as
It tries to steal his life.

There's somethin' that a cowboy knows,
A need he can't explain
That draws him to the soul-fulfilling
Freedom of the plain.

He knows the sound, the siren song—
The coyote's haunting cry—
That makes him roam the wild land
Until his last good-by.

THE DEATH OF JUAN CHACON

FIN BAYLES

The eastern sky was growing light,
The stars were turning pale,
The dawn would chase the shadows
From the strange but friendly trail.

His big brown mare was eager,
And willing his little roan;
Three hundred miles northwest he'd ride;
On his errand went Juan Chacon.

News had come south by the grapevine
And very welcome word,
That north of the San Juan River
There were Mormon sheep to herd.

He'd not be gone but a year or two;
It was a most ambitious scheme;
He'd work and save and come home soon
To his delayed and personal dream.

The long leaves turned to pinion
And the pinion turned to sage,
The sagebrush turned to tumbleweeds
In the lonely desert haze.

But there on the far horizon,
Blest by nature's fountains,
Was the landmark which had beckoned him,
The blue Abajo Mountains.*

He went to work for the Mossback outfit,
His talents soon to hone.
The strong and brave New Mexican,
The sheepman, Juan Chacon.

The sheep camp is a lonely place;
A visitor there is seldom;
A cowboy or a lawman
Or a hungry tramp is welcome.

Now, in that very country
Lived a sorry native brat,
Unschooled, untamed, undisciplined,
The ragged "Little Hat."

At first he came a-begging
For a biscuit or some meat,
So Juan Chacon, the gentleman,
Had him to light and eat.

Springtime turned to summer
And summer turned to fall.
The lambs grew up and ewes grew fat
While Juan watched over all.

And then throughout the winter,
Where the tent and bedground* sat,
Came regularly for mutton stew,
The beggar, "Little Hat."

When springtime finally came again
With greenery and new life,
Juan Chacon thought longingly
Of home and son and wife.

And in his mind, he promised
That to his home he'd go
When summer work was finished
But before the flying snow.

The summer passed by slowly
Where Juan Chacon might be;
Was his wife so fair and lovely—
Was his small son two or three?

So when September ended
He came in his best fettle
With his war sack and his camp stuff,
His wages for to settle.

He settled up his small accounts;
For his kin, bought this and that.
For his wife he bought a white lace shawl,
For himself, a new felt hat.

He packed his faithful little roan;
His big brown mare he sat;
He bid farewell to Utah friends—
Seen by the coward, "Little Hat."

Excitement filled the peaceful air
As he took the trail for home—
A trail which was bound to end too soon
For the traveler, Juan Chacon.

When he finally stopped that night
For some supper and his bed,
A horseman passed far to the right
To seek the trail ahead.

Long before the daylight came,
On his mare with his little roan,
Came an eager, happy, homebound man
On his journey, Juan Chacon.

In the canyon Yellowjacket,*
Which Juan would have to cross,
Came a rider way ahead of him
On a worn-out, jaded horse.

As noon came to the canyon
'Neath the roots of an old dead snag,
A gunman looked at Juan Chacon
Down the sights of a Jorgensen Krag.

Juan lit for a drink of water
And to rest his roan and mare,
When the blast of a big bore rifle
Shattered the noonday air.

The slug took Juan in the kidney,
Through from right to left.
He fell on his face in the shallow creek,
Working hard for breath.

He struggled vainly in the mud;
His death was slow and terrible:
His mouth was full of blood
And his belly full of gravel.

The noon grew long and silence came
And the horses began a-grazin',
And up there in the hawk's nest
The assassin was a-waitin'.

The shadows were a-growin' long
A'fore he caught up with the mare and roan
And then turned his attention
To the corpse of Juan Chacon.

In northern Arizona,
Later that same fall,
A stranger paid a saloon bill
With a white lace shawl.

He bought a meal of mutton stew
With Juan Chacon's new hat,
Then left town on a big brown mare,
The murderer, "Little Hat."

And over in New Mexico
A Mexican gal's a-pinin'
for Juan Chacon to hurry home;
A brown-eyed boy's a-whinin'.

Maybe they're a-thinkin'
'Bout things that might be said,
But they're never gonna get the chance
'Cause Juan Chacon is dead.

Abajo Moutains near Blanding, southeastern Utah, also
known as the Blue Mountains
bedground place where a herd of sheep is bedded each
night, sort of home ground
Yellowjacket a canyon in the Abajo Mountains

SALOONS

ED BROWN

I've been known to spend time in barrooms,
　　Call 'em saloons if you choose,
But whether I stay and spend all my pay
　　Depends on lots more than the booze.

Now I don't go to town all that often,
　　From the ranch it seems really quite far.
But if I'm to return less the few bucks I've earned
　　Depends on who's behind that bar.

If there's an old boy in an apron,
　　Who's friendly but white as a sheet,
I'll have a few drafts and maybe some laughs
　　And wander on off down the street.

If I stay 'til my pockets are empty,
　　Then borrow and beg and write checks,
You can bet that the gender of the bartender
　　Is one of the opposite sex.

If I walk in and she lets out "Howdy,
　　Have a seat, Tex, I'm glad that yer here,"
Even though my name's Buck, I feel I'm in luck,
　　And I'm stuck from the very first beer.

She may be a shade short of gorgeous,
　　Maybe run hard and put away wet,
But if she sounds sincere with what I want to hear
　　I ain't met one that I don't like yet.

When I go broke and swear not to come back,
　　I know that those are useless vows,
'Cuz that old bar gal's face just can't be replaced
　　By the back end of these danged old cows.

COWDOGS

ED BROWN

Now some cowdogs have pedigrees
    And other claims to fame.
But here a cowdog gets two things:
    A whipping and a name.

And we don't just give them a name
    From a book upon the shelves.
We use them, and if they stay around,
    We let them name themselves.

Now Lucky got his easily,
    We didn't like the sound.
He just hopped in the pickup truck
    While I was at the pound.

And Romeo, he's not much show;
    His usefulness is slim.
But all the pups for miles around
    Look exactly like him.

Just how Ol' Screech got his name,
    I bet I beat you to it—
It's the sound that a fence makes
    When he's running cattle through it.

With Ornery's disposition you'd not
    Give him half a chance,
But he does come in handy
    Keeping salesmen off the ranch.

Some of the names that we've bestowed
    Don't need much explanation;
Meter Maid marks tires, and
    Lazy's on vacation.

Backhoe fills the yard with holes;
    Nixon covers them up;
Welfare hasn't done a thing
    Since he was just a pup.

Buzzard eats the darndest things;
    Leppie's mother never claimed him.
If we had a dog that could work cows
    We wouldn't know what to name him.

RANCHERS' REVENGE

BOB CHRISTENSEN

We'd worked all day a-branding calves
And now we took a rest.
Buck opened up a six-pack,
Took a smoke out of his vest.

We started in to contemplate
The problems of the day.
Some stretched out on feed sacks,
Some on a pile of hay.

"You know," he says, "for thirty years
I've been a-running steers,
And how this cattle ranching's changed
Could bring a man to tears.

"Some people say that beef's too high,
Some say it causes cancer;
Any bureaucrat you ask
Will have a different answer.

"And when I think of government
And all the funds they've spent
To get the public on our range,
And then they raised the rent.

"They pay a man to raise no corn;
They buy another's cheese;
They pay you not to milk your cows
And to turn loose half your bees.

"Then Pete says on the radio
They broadcast Tuesday night
That there are just too many cows:
That is the rancher's plight.

"He said some feller took a count—
And don't this 'beat the band'—
He says there are nine million cows
That live upon this land."

Now Joe, he done some ciphering
And then said, "Boys, look here,
What if all of those nine million head
Was one gigantic steer?

"That critter'd weigh a million ton;
He'd reach from coast to coast;
He'd eat 90,000 ton of hay.
But what I like the most—

"He'd have his off hind foot near Buffalo,
The front one in Tacoma,
The near hind hoof in Jacksonville,
The fourth one near Pomona

"And after he ate all that hay,
Wouldn't it raise a fuss
If that steer did to Washington
What Washington's done to us!"

'TIL I DEPART

JOHN DOFFLEMEYER

Few men feel these hillsides breathe
or hear the heartbeat underneath,
'cept those that live here day to day
and nature's beasts can hardly say

a thing. they, like me, tend to slip
to spots just outside most men's grip
and silent watch to stay alive,
and gettin' by, means to survive

any way you can. there ain't no laws
ev'r wrote by man not full of flaws
for moneyed men bound on makin' more.
and i reckon i'm partly tore

between Ma Nature's firm embrace
and those that gain to scar her face,
by findin' ways to live between
that some might judge to be obscene;

i've taken sides against most men,
and hope st. peter finds a pen
where i might be separated,
with the untamed that He created

and turned out next to eden's gate,
(i don't 'spect no perfect state),
just to be what can't be here,
with those that keep Her heartbeat dear.

the pearly gates and towns of gold
don't fit my dreams and could not hold
me long. so i'll keep slippin' by,
the way i've done until i die;

and if smokin' don't take my breath
or a fallen horse crush me to death,
or cholest'rol don't plug my heart
i'll keep on rhymin' 'til i depart.

DROUGHT OF SEVENTY-SEVEN

JOHN DOFFLEMEYER

It was dry in the fall of seventy-six
and the cows were a calvin' in the dust,
nothin' to see but acres of chips,
a drought year where cowmen went bust.

their hides were rough 'n' just cover'd bone
'n' ribs caught most of your eye,
spindly calves seemed to wander alone,
as if lookin' for a place to die.

cows were bringin' two-bits a pound,
a hundred bucks less than the spring,
all ya could do, was throw hay on the ground,
and pray to God it would rain.

their toes would clack like castanets
in the cloud that'd boil 'round your truck,
the bawlin' skeletons and weak silhouettes
would bring tears to the drought of good luck.

reckon Ma Nature's
showed me who's boss,
as she'll do some time and again,
but she's never caused me half of the loss
that politicians create with a pen.

BLACKROCK PASS

JOHN DOFFLEMEYER

A thunderstorm began to form
with a hat-sized cloud in the pass,
'lectricity charged the horses' manes
on this spiritual spot for mass.

we'd fished the kern at funston,
when one would feed all four
and buck would pick a tune to sing,
back some years—at least a score.

ezra brooks and a flickerin' fire
beneath a billion coals above,
cut by the silhouette of the swayin' pines,
and winkin' as the pine needles moved.

dan gave us things to think about
and john challenged the river,
buck gave me music for my songs,
that packin' mules 'llows one to deliver.

we pulled our slickers on
and baled off the western slope
and at the second switchback
zeus* tossed his yellow rope

not too far from where we paused
and roared in the canyon walls,
then tossed another to the other side
and loose rocks began to fall.

we felt like calves in a brandin' pen
and it began to pour;
buck asked me if we'd live,
and chilled us to the core.

buck began with "our fathers..."
and followed with the twenty-third psalm,
hunched on that cottontail mule,
alternatin' as we went along.

at cyclamen* and columbine,*
more ropers tried their luck,
boulders fell from both sides
mor'n' 'nuff to fill a truck.

dan moved steady down,
havin' calculated the odds,
john grinned that smile of his,
almost laughin' at the gods.

my cotton lead was stiff and wet,
with rivers runnin' off my brim,
buck had increased his volume,
as we took turns joinin' in.

we finally made pinto lake
to dry beneath the fly,
and i'll wager these successful men
would like to return as much as i.

Zeus head Greek mythological deity adept at tossing light-
ning bolts
Cyclamen and Columbine two lakes on the west slope of
Blackrock Pass, Tulare County, Sequoia National Park,
California

LISTEN TO THE SUN GO DOWN

LEON FLICK

Upon a warm September's eve,
the sun was dipping low.
I sat myself upon a rim,
from there to watch the show.

The shadows were their longest now,
as darkness soon would be.
I closed my eyes and listened
to the sounds I couldn't see.

The quail chatted nervously,
about to go to bed.
The hoot-owl screeched a different tune,
his whole night lay ahead.

The rock chuck whistled one last cry,
and from his warm rock he did slide.
The deer crept from the willows,
no longer there to hide.

The coyote howled from up on top,
before his nightly quest.
The wasps that had been buzzing
were now safe within their nest.

The magpie and the meadowlark
and rooster pheasant too,
All said, "see you in the morning,"
and off to roost they flew.

The bobcat didn't say much
as he tested out the air.
The porcupine wandered to the creek
to get a drink from there.

The nighthawks were coming about to life,
after hiding all day from the sun.
The muskrat and the beaver splashed,
Either working or having fun.

And I can promise you one thing,
you will smile instead of frown
If you'll close your eyes and open your ears
and listen to the sun go down.

GO AND JUST BUCKAROO

LEON FLICK

They say with barbed wire came the fall of the West,
I ain't denyin' it's true.
'Cuz there's few places left, in this once empty West,
you can go and just buckaroo.

But you follow a fence and you'll find gate or hole,
and there you can wander on through.
But the days are gone, when you took horse and tack,
and could go and just buckaroo.

For the East runs this land, and they don't
    understand
about cows or our points of view.
They don't even care if they're playin' square,
or care 'bout some lost buckaroo.

But throw the gate wide, 'cuz I'm still full of pride,
and I'll fight 'em till my life is through.
And out in the West, when they lay me to rest,
I'll go and just buckaroo.

A WHAT??!!

KAY KELLEY

The honeymoon was in full swing.
We settled in in Santa Fe.
This cowgirl starting a brand new life
After our wedding day.

I'd been picked up in the pasture
By my handsome 'Man of the West.'
One early morn, I questioned him
While cuddled in our love nest.

"You had told me you're a big ranchowner
Back when you were courting me.
Well, now that the wedding's over
Those ranches I'd like to see."

"Why sure," he said, "I'll be right back."
As he leaped out of the bed.
"This here's my 36-inch wrench.
The 24's are in the shed."

"A *wrench*owner is what you meant?"
I choked in disbelief.
"Yes, I'm a Master Plumber."
His pride added to my grief.

Now, my heroes had all been cowboys
That stirred my romantic soul.
And I had never seen John Wayne
Playing a plumber's role.

Trying to restore the faith in him
This revelation began to destroy,
I asked him about Joe Lemon's ranch
Where he'd worked summers as a boy.

"How many cows did Joe Lemon run?"
"Two—two milking Holsteins."
"No, how many cows out on the range
Where you cowboyed in your teens?"

"Oh, it was a sheep ranch," he replied.
My heart went numb in shock.
"I married a sheep-herding plumber!"
The shriek could be heard for blocks.

Too late to run, the vow was made,
I tried to carry on.
When friends would ask, "How's married life?"
My answer was, "I was conned."

'The Sting' wasn't in it with my guy.
He'd employed every trick and ruse.
His morals and scruples were shiny clean,
They never had been used.

Through the years I've come to know him well,
As we lope through life together.
I've ridden many a mile with him
In both good and stormy weather.

The honeymoon's still in full swing
He's my partner and best friend.
I'm thankful now that I got conned.
Things worked out best in the end.

So I'll stick with my sheep-herding plumber
Right into eternity.
For 'he'll do to ride the river with'
And he sure is special to me.

TREASURE

KAY KELLEY

When I cowboyed for the old ZR
I thought my job was great.
We raised good Hereford range bulls
That were known throughout the state.

I was the top hand on the ranch,
At least next to my dog, Shep.
You see, I was the only hand.
That's how I got that rep.

The boss brought home a high-powered bull.
From Doolittle's Sale he came.
Golden Treasure L588
And as fancy as his name.

Two thousand eighty on the scales,
In the trap, we turned him loose.
A classic model of the Hereford breed,
Traits we hoped he'd reproduce.

Though Treas was an independent bull,
And let his chips fall where they may,
He'd been on the show string* when he was young.
He was gentle, and I liked to play.

So I made a pet out of that bull,
And he'd patiently tolerate
All my fussing when I fed him.
I even rode him while he ate.

After two weeks in the little trap,
Eating grain up near the house,
It was time to put Treas with the cows,
But that bull just wouldn't chouse.

He'd ignore my horse and whipping rope,
'Til the boss and I agreed
I'd have to take him up there on foot
Since he was broke to lead.

His curly head in a halter,
Well, this time he didn't balk.
It felt like taking a giant
One-ton poodle for a walk.

Our trip was uneventful
'Til that bull became aroused.
He struck a long, determined trot.
Old Treas had smelled the cows.

Where I come from, the unwritten rule
Was you never do let go.
So through the brush and cholla thorns
That bull had me in tow.

Scrambling over rocks and bushes with
Falling down among my fears,
I desperately hollered, "heel!"
But it fell upon deaf ears.

We found the cows up on the ridge.
Our final mile was run.
I slipped the halter off his head
As he covered the nearest one.

So let's hear it for tradition,
The cowboy mounted on his steed,
The old ways are the best ways.
Bulls were meant to drive, not lead!

show string fairs and stock shows

PLAYING WITH FOXY'S NOSE

KAY KELLEY

I have a bay cutting filly
That can sure scowl at a cow.
You'd be impressed by her classy moves
If you saw her sweep and bow.
But when we're not working cattle,
Where she has to be quick on her toes,
A quiet pleasure we both enjoy
Is playing with Foxy's nose.

As I stroke her fluttering nostrils
And our breaths we do exchange,
She smells of sweet alfalfa
And the grasses of the range.
And looking up into big, brown eyes,
Her concentration shows
Just how intent she is on our game,
While I'm playing with Foxy's nose.

Her strip flows down along her face
And puddles in a snip.
As I hold her velvet muzzle,
She never tries to nip.
So we share these peaceful moments,
While my filly snorts and blows.
Each breathing in contentment,
While we're playing with Foxy's nose.

BRANDS

MIKE LOGAN

Me an' Slim was movin' heifers
Down Highway 33.
When this Cadillac with New York plates
Pulls up beside o' me.

The lady driver, she leans out
An' waves to me an' him.
Then purty soon she's drivin' 'long
An' talkin' with ol' Slim.

She asks 'im 'bout the cowboy life
An' 'bout his hoss an' such.
An' why them bulls is wearin' stars.
It's plain she don't know much.

"Well, ma'am, them stars is brands," Slim says.
"They tell who owns the cow."
She asks him, "Are there many brands?"
That lady's done it now!

Ol' Slim don't usu'lly talk too much,
But he gets plumb wound up!
Ya' get 'im talkin' cattle brands
He's eager as a pup!

"Why, ma'am, you bet!! There's quite a few!!"
Ol' Slim builds to the task.
"Could you just name a few of them?"
I hear that lady ask.

"Shoot, ma'am, I'd be right happy to!"
He takes a mighty breath.
That lady's in grave danger
O' plumb bein' talked to death!

Ol' Slim, he starts off kind o' slow
Then steams right on ahead.
An' best as I can recollect
These brands is ones he said.

"There's Broken Hearts and Lazy K's
An Muleshoes an' Walkin' A's.
There's Runnin' W's, Tumblin' T's
An' Bar B Q's an' Di'mond 3's.

"There's X Bar M's an' Rockin' R's
An' Turkey Tracks an' Circle Stars.
There's Y Bar 5's an' Rafter P's
An' Triangles an' Slash N C's.

"There's Broken Arrows, Risin' Suns
An' Tomahawks an' 1 Bar 1's.
There's Quarter Moons an' Backward E's
An' I O U's an' Twin Pine Trees.

"There's Six Shooters an' Z Bar N's
An' Question Marks an' Number 10's.
There's Pick an' Shovels, Double G's
An' Quarter Circle Crazy B's.

"There's Candlesticks an' Open A's
An' Arrowheads an' Hanging J's.
There's Anchors an' a Triple Cross
An' even some shaped like a Hoss.

"There's Pitchers, Teapots an' there's Cups
An' Wineglasses an' 7 Ups.
There's Cloverleafs an' Mission Bells
An' Eyeglasses an' Schoolboy L's.

"There's Top Hats an' there's Buttonhooks
An' lots that's hard to read in books.
There's Box F's an the 4 T 4
An', by gum, ma'am, there's plenty more."

Ol' Slim, he's soundin' windbroke,
His breath's a comin' rough.
His face is turnin' beet red.
This namin' brands is tough!!

"You mean you haven't named them all?"
That lady cain't but stare.
"Why, I ain't hardly started, ma'am.
I just run out o' air!"

AN ANCIENT BEAVERSLIDE

MIKE LOGAN

Alone it stood,
All made of wood,
Hip deep in drifted snow.
Of lodgepole pines
And jutting tines,
Its ribs all seemed to show.

In bygone times
And gentler climes,
It used to stack wild hay.
But nature's rage
And ripe old age
Had placed it there to stay.

Gray arms held high
To touch the sky,
It seemed some fossiled beast
That rose to fight,
To claw and bite
And froze there, facing east.

Its weathered bones
Seemed turned to stones
That, long since, petrified.
It was, in fact,
Though broken backed,
An ancient beaverslide.*

beaverslide part of a particular type of hay-
stacking equipment; see illustration

OL' COOKY

MIKE LOGAN

Now, Ol' Cooky was some ugly
An' he surely weren't no rose.
If you lost him in a stampede
You could find him with your nose.

Cooky wasn't scared of water.
Shoot, he used it ever' day
Makin' coffee, beans and biscuits,
But wash in it? No way!!!

Now, I ain't faultin' Cooky.
He could sure 'nuff rustle grub.
But he'd get just plain insulted
At the mention of a tub.

Cooky's apple pie was heaven,
It just seemed some angel's blend.
Punchers purt' near fought for seconds,
But they always ate upwind.

Cooky's wagon, it was spotless.
Plates and cups was shiny clean.
But you just mention bathin'
An' Ol' Cooky'd get plumb mean.

You really cain't blame Cooky.
He only had one shirt.
We never knowed which parts was cloth
An' which parts grease and dirt.

I roped a skunk for Cooky once.
Just did it for a joke!!
When I drug him up to Cooky,
Well, I thought that skunk'd choke.

We lost Ol' Cooky that year,
At a crossin' on the Platte;
Chuckwagon tipped in midstream.
We only found his hat.

Ol' Cooky never learned to swim.
A fact too late found out.
'Course, I always thought if watered right
Ol' Cooky'd prob'ly sprout.

He's likely makin' pine trees now,
With needles long and green.
He lived his life in one old shirt,
But he met his Maker clean.

A COWBOYIN' DAY

GARY McMAHAN

Morning is just a thin line to the east
as you steps in the corral and captures a beast;
cold saddle blankets, cock-a-doodle-doo;
don't buck now, you bugger, you'll break me in two.

And your head starts workin' on the last pass around;
saddle horses are wrangled, draft horses cut out;
you shuts the gate and steps to the ground;
it's hot black coffee you're thinking 'bout now.

Then biscuits and gravy and eggs over light;
and the foreman's wife is a beautiful sight;
jokes and jabs and the cowboss's* orders;
a chew and a toothpick and you're out the door.

To saddle the horse you'll use for the day,
making sure your riggin' has no extra play,
you steps aboard light with him all gathered up,
for you know firsthand the critter can buck.

Ease him out at a walk, head north towards the
     dump;
you'll be askin' a trot when he loses his hump;
you hits a slow lope on the badger highway;
it's a cool mornin' blue sky cowboyin' day.

And the brooks are babbling down through the holes,
the meadowlarks sing the song in your soul,
the wildflowers blaze any color you s'pose,
as the smell of sagebrush and pine fill your nose.

Now the horse that you're on is big and lean,
quick, tough, smart, and a little bit mean;
his saddle's no place for the meek or green;
he's a sho'nuff ripsnortin' cowboyin' machine.

And the place that you're headed is pretty intense;
continental divide is the back fence;
there's 10,000 acres of mountain and rock there,
and 1,200 head to check to the doctor.

And to make matters worse—or better, you think,
they're all yearling heifers, unpredictable dinks;
they'll run and hide till hell freezes twice,
then kick up their heels as you skate on the ice.

But this ain't no colt and you ain't no kid,
so you jerks out your rope and pulls down your lid,
and climbs and cruises the sagebrush and aspen,
till you finds a cowbrute* what's droopy and raspin'.

And you tags her just 'fore she gets to the brush,
then trips her and ties her in a big rush,
packs her with sulfa and penicillin;
she'll turn for the better, good Lord a-willin'.

Lots of foot rot and pinkeye today,
but that don't mean the buggers can't play;
they've ducked and dodged till who laid a chunk,*
but you managed to capture a pretty good hunk.

A line-backed heifer with a sly side dart
almost upset the whole apple cart;
and a bald-faced old bag sure slammed on the brakes
when we dived off a ledge and got in her way.

It's the heat of the day now, sun's straight overhead,
and you and your horse is packin' some lead;
you hanker for rest and a biscuit or two,
and you figgers you got that much comin' to you.

Your horse likes the grass that grows 'neath the
    aspen,
and the shade there is welcome as peace everlastin';
so you find such a place with a creek close by
to sooth the bruises of a hard ride.

You hobbles,* unbridles him, loosens his girth,
then sets yourself back in the cool green earth,
surrounds your grub and drinks your fill
and takes a siesta way back in the hills.

A catnap is all you require,
still you lay there and ponder a thought:
the world sure has its briars.
take for instance this good old cowhoss.

He was a wide-eyed, ring-tailed dandy.
They give up on him 'fore they give him to me.
but it's same for horses as it is for men:
he just needed a job and a kick in the shin.

The afternoon's spent with the usual flair,
a close call here, a catastrophe there;
but still you saved more than a couple of hides;
that's why you get paid for makin' these rides.

A storm blew through for about thirty minutes,
and you'd swear that Satan hisself was in it;
you're sure glad your pony is seasoned plumb through;
close lightning's unloaded a few buckaroos.

You're wet as a fish, but you ain't gonna melt,
and the sun feels the best it ever has felt;
you're all steamed up like an overdo freight,
but you're dry as a duck time you get to the gate.

Now they's those thinks a cowboy's a crude, ignorant
    cuss;
truth is, we no-savvy them that no-savvy us;
but there's one chore that sticks in my mind,
when a cowboy's job cuts into sublime.

When you and your horse form a leathery feather,
and drift two-three yearlings—out of a gather
and trail 'em up someplace they don't want to go,
when they're needing a vet or whatever, y'know.

You set 'em just so when you go through a gate,
and don't rile 'em up, for heaven's sake;
those that have tried it say it's kinda an art
to pen 'em in the home corral before dark.

And you're trailin' two of them home this night;
we'll probably ship* one, the other'll be alright;
but one wrong move now, the air's turnin' cool,
and these two yearlins'll make you look like a fool.

You punch 'em into the catch with a whoop and a
      smile;
you've been walkin' on eggs for the last few miles,
and if one woulda broke the fur woulda flew;
no tellin' when you'd get another crack at them two.

Your horse rolls in the dirt while you put up your
      tack,*
then savors his grain as you scratch his back;
it's an evenin' ritual you both enjoy;
you don't covet nothin' when you ride this ol' boy.

And he heads for the timothy down by the lake,
whilst you saunters to the house for soup and steak,
to mix it up with compadres and finish your pie,
like lotsa folks do when they're satisfied.

When supper is done there's little time for play;
you sleep hard all night if you work hard all day;
and 'fore you fall off your log to float in the air,
you may have time for a little prayer.

"Lord, I thank you for this cowboyin' day;
I had me some fun whilst earnin' my pay,
and I like to think I keep meat on the table
for a country that needs to keep fit and able.

"But a cow with no horse, Lord, is boring as hell,
and a horse with no cows don't ring my bell;
it's a good life, this game of Horses and Cattle;
and thanks again, Lord, for my day in the saddle.
Amen."

cowboss the man in charge of the day-to-day workings of
the ranch
cowbrute a cow
who laid a chunk after a hard chase you may find some
manure on the trail . . . you don't know who did it because
things were going by too fast
hobble tie the feet of a horse so he can't run off
ship send to the slaughterers
tack saddle, bridle, and blanket

THE TWO THINGS IN LIFE
THAT I REALLY LOVE

GARY McMAHAN

There's two things in life
That I really love:
That's women and horses,
This I'm sure of.
So when I die,
Please tan my hide
And tool me into
A saddle so fine.
And give me to a cowgirl
Who likes to ride,
So in the hereafter
I may rest
Between the two things
That I love best.

A JOKER'S PAY

ROD McQUEARY

If you can make a week-old prolapse seem
Romantic as a schoolgirl's dream,
Describe the sweet and lovely things
Held together with hog rings,*
You'll deserve your gold "B.S." degree
In western cowboy poetry.

But writing poems, and jokes, and such
For this cattle crowd won't pay too much.
You see, they can't afford to pay to hear
The real value of a dying steer,
Or all about this market mess
That brings on all their money stress
And doubt
About tiny checks toward giant notes,
Worn out overshoes and coats,
Old gloves turned inside out.

Please, don't forget the numbers, friend,
Write those great big numbers down.
All that pretty equity (and fifty cents)
Will buy a cup of coffee
Nearly anywhere in town.

And who here hasn't visualized
That long-dreaded day,
When some sympathetic crowd, somber auctioneer,
Sells your world away?
Some bitter husband, weeping wife,
Decide what now to do with life
Or where to go,
How *not* to feel like failures
At the only thing they know.

So if you write the poems and jokes
To entertain these western folks
Who watch the cows, or herd the sheep,
For their sake, keep it light,
And take the laughter for your pay,
Because right now, tears are cheap.

hog rings metal clips to repair a prolapse; they "hold together" a cow's rear end

---

THE PISTOL

ROD McQUEARY

It's a still and quiet twilight
When the rider comes alone,
Jogging, trotting down a grassy draw
On his lathered, limping roan.

You see, he was making for the valley,
But he knows now, it's too far,
'Cause the Indians have fresh horses,
And he can't hear where they are.

Must have been a hunting party
Out for deer, beyond the butte.
And he never saw them hiding,
Until he heard them shoot.

Now the dribble off his stirrup
Ends the slick and rosy strip
From the bullet in his kidney,
In the hole above his hip.

He'd lost his hat and pack horse.
Their shots broke his saddle gun
And spilled the roan, and wrecked his elbow,
Now there's nowhere left to run.

His last weapon is the pistol,
Old, and heavy—.44.
He took it from a dying major,
A real prize back in the war.

"One of Pennsylvania's finest,"
Back when he was just a kid.
Sometimes the dreams still haunt him,
About the awful things they did.

If he can't make the valley,
And won't see another day,
He won't let them have this pistol;
He'd rather throw his prize away.

He pulls and drops it in the bushes.
The pain just takes away his breath,
So he slips off the roan—real easy,
Curls up, and bleeds to death.

It's several years before they find him—
Just bones and leather, tattered shirt.
And they never see the pistol
Behind the bushes, in the dirt.

Summer evening, 1987,
This same old familiar ground
Wears lush alfalfa windrows
Each time the swather comes around.

Driven by some worried, weary farmer,
The pickup's far, and he can see
He'll be late again for supper
(And he had promised not to be).

That old swather chatters, smoking,
As it climbs up that mound
That some old-timer once had told him
Used to be a battleground.

When one low tire, slick and spinning,
Turns the sickle angle wrong,
It cuts through sod to rusty pistol
That's been laying there so long.

Hard old steel breaks several sections,
And that knocks out some guards.
That farmer knows it's trouble,
'Cause that side is pushing hard.

Beside the matted alfalfa whisker,
Right between the farmer's boots,
Are shiny cuts on a short, corroded pipe
In a gob of rusty roots.

He grabs and throws that evil junk.
It makes the swather slap.
He says, "Damn those darned old-timers!
Why couldn't they pick up this crap?"

HARD MOVE

ROD McQUEARY

They had heard the news, and it was bad.
So neighbors came to help them move;
Dear friends, who came not just to lift,
But to offer all they were, and had—
This kindness—as a farewell gift.

Out here, cash money's slim, and the life is hard,
These rural folks don't vacation much.
And so, there soon will come a day
When a Christmas wish, or birthday card,
Will be all they do to keep in touch,
As the fondness, like the promises,
Slowly melts away.

By some fresh-scrubbed wall, the woman stands;
Hard work's the friend she leans on now.
It's noon, yet she won't eat or sit;
Neither work-worn heart nor calloused hands can quit,
I guess they don't know how.

Her elm tree's just a withered stick;
Starved shadows rake a lawn—long, brown.
High interest rates and four years of drought
Have killed the creek and starved them out.
After this, it won't seem so bad in town.

Neat boxes weight the wagons down,
Sympathetic hands have placed them there—
Possessions so worn and plain and cheap, you wonder
    how,
For such a simple ride like this one to town,
They justify such care.

Drivers fidget as the sun drops back,
When the woman finally comes alone,
And turns to view the sterile shack
With the smoky stove, and the window crack
That used to be ...
Her home.

So she climbs aboard and takes her seat,
And though her eyes are dry,
Still, it is a sad retreat.
Sometimes it's hard to tell a part of life,
And love,
"Goodbye."

HAT ETIQUETTE

WALLACE McRAE

There are rules of decorum and conduct
    to which genuine cowboys attest.
Call them mores, traditions or manners,
    they're part of the code of the West.
But cowpokes have got this dilemma,
    that confuses these sage diplomats.
It involves the whens and when-not-tos,
    concerning the wearing of hats.
The old rule concerning head covers says:
    "Hat-up when you work, or you ride.
Tip 'em to women. But take John B. off
    when in bed, or when you're inside."
But whaddya do in a gin mill,
    bean shops or dances in town?
Where Resistol rustlers'll filch it
    or some lowlife'll puke in its crown.
'N there ain't no such thing as a hat rack
    anyplace that I been of late.
So we all compromise with a tip back,
    baring pallid foreheads and bald pate.

What we need is a new resolution
   to settle this conflict we got.
So I come up with this here solution,
   a result of consider'ble thought:
"I move that we do like good Hebrews,
   wear hats from our birth 'til we die.
And never remove them sombreros.
   All those in favor say, 'Aye.' "

GRANDMOTHER'S FRENCH HOLLYHOCKS

WALLACE McRAE

They were probably planted there by the gate
Or along the fence of the watergap lot,
Where the milk cows lazed and the work teams ate,
Chicken-wired out of the garden plot.

Why, didn't she know they'd scatter around,
Their seeds infecting our vegetable garden?
Magenta blooms fought for fertile ground,
Crowding and choking, begging no pardon

Of the carrots or beets in militant rows,
Cut down by the shrapnel of Gaulish* genes,
From ambush, they fell like dominoes.
In retreat we skirmished to save the beans

For the canning jars, waiting empty and green,
Wide-mouthed as grackles with demanding maws
That would nourish during months snowy and lean,
When the hunger moon, grinning, flexed grizzled jaws.

"Foolish woman!" we thought, to be tempted by beauty.
"What could she be thinking?" so all of us said.
Our lives bound by the iron bands of duty,
Not frivolous flowers! Just beans, beef and bread.

Of course, no one complained (not to her face).
She surely repented the sin of her ways.
Her silent apology mitigated disgrace,
But the shame of her weakness she bore all her days.

She was guilty, of course—more guilty were we.
For beauty in life has strong healing powers.
Fifty years later, I'm beginning to see
The value of Grandmother's beautiful flowers.

Gaulish meaning French

GIVE US A SONG, IAN TYSON

WALLACE McRAE

Write me a tune, Ian Tyson,*
With a beat sort of easy and slow,
That will flow down each valley and canyon
From Alberta to Old Mexico.
Make it sound like the wind in the pine trees
Or the plains muffled deep in the snow.
Yes, please, write me a tune, Ian Tyson,
Like an old one the cowboys all know.

Write down some words, Ian Tyson,
Words that put a sad tear in my eye.
Words that speak of the unspoken yearning
That I have for the old days gone by.
Tell again of our shame, or our glory,
With a shout, or perhaps with a sigh.
Won't you write down some words, Ian Tyson,
Of the West, 'neath a big open sky?

Sing me your song, Ian Tyson,
Would you sing your song only for me?
Let the ripples of music transport me
Like the waves carry ships on the sea.
Make me fight, or just languidly listen.
Sing of strife, or of sweet harmony.
But please sing me your song, Ian Tyson,
Sing it softly and easy and free.

Teach us your song, Ian Tyson,
So the cowboys can all sing along.
And forgive when we stumble and mumble,
Or we get the verses all wrong.
It's your fate to be placed as the hero
Of a bowlegged buckaroo throng.
So we'll borrow your song, Ian Tyson,
And then call it our own cowboy song.

They'll steal your song, Ian Tyson,
Steal the song that the cowboys love well,
And they'll change both the beat and the lyrics,
Then they'll merchandise it with hard sell.
Let the Nashvillains ride plastic ponies
Round and round on their fake carousel.
Yet your song will remain on the ranches
Of the West, where the true cowboys dwell.

Thanks for your song, Ian Tyson,
For the ballad that crept from your pen.
Out here into our hearts in the heartland,
To the home of the true saddlemen.
For we're weary tonight of the strident,
Of the tedious rock regimen.
So, please sing one more time, Ian Tyson,
Your song. Yes, sing it again.

Ian Tyson, a Canadian performer, is the author's (and
probably the cowboys') favorite cowboy singer and song
writer.

Dedicated to the memory of my uncle Evan D. McRae

OUTRIDERS AT THE END OF THE TRAIL

WALLACE McRAE

They contemplate their town-boot toes
As they stand around and mill.
They check the south horizon,
'Cross the tracks above the hill.
Their suitcoats hint of mothballs.
Their Levis are clean and creased.
They speak of grass or cattle
But never the deceased.
Some have shook the Gov'nor's hand,
And one's been in the pen.
Crooked legs define the bronc hands,
Cropped off thumbs the dally men.
Their springtoothed necks are throttled up
In silky black wild rags.
Their faces scored like flower-stamps
On well-worn saddle bags.
They've come early to the funeral home,
Yet don't want to go inside.
There's no comfort in a breathless room
Or words of "eventide."
They somehow share a secret bond
As each one recollects:
Together.   Separate.   Silently.
Each pays his last respects.

You'll hear no keening to the vaulted skies,
But the good hands know when a good hand dies.

THE YELLOWSTONE

WALLACE McRAE

Millions of buffalo curried her flanks
    as she shed winter's ice in the spring.
In the smoke of ten thousand campfires
    she heard drum beats and war dances ring.
On the crest of her bosom, she sped Captain Clark
    and Sacajawea as well.
She bisected prairie, the plains and the mountains
    from her birthplace in "John Colter's Hell."
To the trav'ler she whispered, "Come follow me,"
    with a wink and a toss of her head.
She tempted the trapper, gold miner and gambler
    to lie down by her sinuous bed.
"Safe passage," she murmured provocatively.
    "Safe passage and riches as well."
She smiled as the thread of Custer's blue line
    followed her trails and then fell.
She carved out the grade for the railroads;
    took settlers to their new home;
Watered their stock, watered the fields,
    and let them grow crops on her loam.
Her banks were the goal of the trail herds.
    Her grass was the prize that they sought.
Till the blizzards of 'eighty-six and seven
    nearly killed off the whole lot.
"Don't boss her, don't cross her." Let her run free,
    and damn you don't dam her at all.
She's a wild old girl, let her looks not deceive you . . .
    But we love her in spite of it all.

THINGS OF INTRINSIC WORTH

WALLACE McRAE

Remember that sandrock on Emmells Crick
Where Dad carved his name in 'thirteen?
It's been blasted down into rubble
And interred by their dragline machine.
Where Fadhls lived, at the old Milar Place,
Where us kids stole melons at night?
They 'dozed it up in a funeral pyre
Then torched it. It's gone alright.
The "C" on the hill, and the water tanks
Are now classified "reclaimed land."
They're thinking of building a golf course
Out there, so I understand.
The old Egan Homestead's an ash pond
That they say is eighty feet deep.
The branding corral at the Douglas Camp
Is underneath a spoil heap.
And across the crick is a tipple, now,
Where they load coal onto a train.
The Mae West Rock on Hay Coulee?
Just black and white snapshots remain.
There's a railroad loop and a coal storage shed
Where the bison kill site used to be.
The Guy Place is gone; Ambrose's too.
Beulah Farley's ranch refugee.

But things are booming. We've got this new school
That's envied across the whole state.
When folks up and ask, "How's things goin' down
     there?"
I grin like a fool and say, "Great!"
Great God, how we're doin'! We're rollin' in dough,
As they tear and they ravage The Earth.
And nobody knows ... or nobody cares ...
About things of intrinsic worth.

THE WHOLE LOAD

WADDIE MITCHELL

In a western town in the days of old,
'Fore the mines closed down for the lack of gold,
The folks there seized opportunity
An' built them a right smart community.
They built 'em a school where the R's were taught,
An' they built them a church on a corner lot;
They painted her white, with a steeple high
To greet townfolk as they's passin' by.

They had 'em a sheriff, a judge an' a mayor,
But they needed a preacher to make things square.
So they sent back East, as was the general rule,
An' hired one fresh from divinity school.
When Sunday come he was all decked out
To preach his sermon, whisper an' shout.
But when he stepped out to the podium,
It was all too obvious that no one come

'Cept one old cowboy in a pew back there,
In his Sunday shirt an' his greased-down hair.
He sat there quiet, just watched the floor,
With a 'ccasional glance towards the church's door.
Time stood still for the longest while,
Till the preacher coughed an' faked a smile:
"Guess we could try it again next week."
But emotion reigned; he could hardly speak.

His demeanor was that of a scolded pup.
He turned to leave when ol' Jake spoke up:
"Hold on there, Parson, it taint yer fault,
An' them thar doors ain't like no vault,
'Cuz thar ain't locks for to keep folks out;
An' if you don't preach now, Satan's won the bout.
Now if I was t' haul out a whole load o' hay,
An' only one cow showed, she'd get fed that day."

Well, this preachin' man, in the last few days,
Found it hard to cope with the western ways.
But he figured as how he'd found his call
From this profound man with his western drawl.
So he fixed his collar an' he stood up straight
And commenced to expound on the pearly gates;
And he shocked himself at his own recall
Of the book he waved, chapter, verse an' all.

It was God Almighty's omnipotent power
That he lectured on for near an hour,
Then the wages of sin an' the hell's brim fire;
An' he didn't weaken an' he didn't tire.
He was jumpin' an' screamin' an' poundin' the floor,
When he noticed ol' Jake weren't awake anymore.
Now, this made him mad, and he stomped to the pew;
He shook Jake's shoulder an' he said, "I'm not through.

"You're the one told me 'bout the cow gettin' fed,
An' here you're a-actin' like you're home in bed."
"You're right there, Preach, 'bout the things I told you;
If I'd a load of hay it would still stand true:
That cow would get fed, 'tis the cowboy's code—
But I wouldn't feed her the whole durn load."

SOLD YOUR SADDLE

WADDIE MITCHELL

Not so terribly well, I said, in answer to his question.
I'm running fast, but I wonder if it's in the wrong
    direction.
My wife has started gainin' weight and gray shows in
    her hair.
Her existence seems to be in runnin' kids from here
    to there.
My job has lost its challenge, seems like it never
    changes.
Sometimes I want to chuck it all and leave to ride
    new ranges.

I thought my friend would understand, he'd walked
    this same old road,
And made decisions in his life to drop his heavy load.
So, I laid my troubles on him and I told him how I felt.
He just stares at me all hollow, like he's hit below the belt.
He sits down close all weak-like, and he looks me in the eye;
His hands, they started tremblin'; I thinks he's gonna cry.

He swallows hard and tells me, "I know what you're up
    against.
It happens at this time of life, you feel like you've been
    fenced.
Seems like life becomes routine, it all just seems the same.
So, you go to huntin' witches, lookin' for someone to
    blame.
Our work and wife scapegoat real well when we are of that
    mind,
And little faults become big 'cuz that's what we want to
    find.

"Don't make my same mistake and let a notion be
   your guide;
The grass ain't greener, I see that now I'm on the
   other side.
I've upturned several lives with my leavin', plus my
   own,
And lost my common little family and my routine
   little home.
I'd have never left if I'd taken time to figure out
That what I wanted out of is what life is all about.

"We're seldom taught that, though; seems it's almost
   out of style.
If I could just have one more chance, I'd walk that
   extra mile.
But that can't be, so I must lie upon the bed I've
   made,
While my will to carry on, like bad memories, start to
   fade.
And if you never take advice again, please, heed these
   words, my friend:
The purpose to life's race is in the runnin' to the
   end.

"Oh, they'll be times it seems so far we feel we'll
   never make it.
We tire and lose sight of dreams and want to just
   forsake it.
It's still all in your mind right now, but thought
   precedes the act,
And it isn't yet too late, my friend, I know that for
   a fact.
You've started your race gamely; you've just been
   bumped against the rail.
I'm not sayin' you sold your saddle, but you've put
   it up for sale."

STORY WITH A MORAL

WADDIE MITCHELL

Now I know there's things worse that make cowpunchers
   curse,
And I reckon it's happened to us all.
Though it's years since, you bet, when I think of it yet,
It still makes my old innards crawl.

I was makin' a ride to bring in one hide
That hadn't showed up in the gather;
I was riding upstream, daydreamin' a dream,
When I caught there was somethin' the matter.

Near some quakin' asp trees, I had caught in the breeze
A stench that was raunchy and mean,
And I reckoned as how it might be the old cow,
So I rode to a bend in the stream.

Shore 'nuff that cow lied in the crick there and died;
Hard tellin' how long she'd been there.
She was bloated and tight, twas a horrible sight—
She was oozin' and slippin' her hair.

Her eye sockets were alive with maggots that thrive
On dead flesh, putrid yellow and green,
And the hot sun burnin' down, turnin' pink things to
   brown,
Spewin' oily gunk in the stream.

Well, I spurred upwind fast to get away from the blast
Of the heavy stench the cow made;
And I felt bad seein's how I'd lost the ol' cow,
And I pulled up near a tree in the shade.

Then I got sick to the core, rememberin' just minutes
   before
I'd done something that made me feel worse:
Not thirty yards down I'd stepped off to the ground
And drank 'til my belly near burst.

For months after it, just the thought made me spit,
And I'd live it over like a bad dream.
And the moral, I think, is if you *must* take a drink,
Never, ever remount and ride upstream.

BIRTH OF A NATIVE TEXAN

BARNEY NELSON

I'm here to say I'm Texican from my hat down to my
  boot,
And whenever folks are braggin', on the Texas horn I
  toot.
Now it hasn't always been this way, my loyalty's
  kinda new,
But let me tell my story; you'll understand before I'm
  through.

I grew up in Arizona, where the manzanita grows;
I paid my dues with shredded shirt, skint hands and
  busted toes.
I rolled the rocks 'round Bagdad,* near Mayer*
  escaped sure death,
And on Aravipa Canyon's wild trails I held my breath.

Not that I was much a hand, no oil wells there, you see,
So they accepted all free help, even green as me.
When twigs popped there, you never knew if made from
  flight or fight,
But I did my best, a-ridin' hard, just to keep their dust
  in sight.

Then fate dealt me a funny hand, made me a Texas
  bride.
And through those Arizona hills, no more was I to
  ride.
My husband was a patient man, treated colts and
  women kind,
And never said my braggin' ways was heavy on his
  mind.

I told him 'bout the Ericksons* and the wild ones
    they brought out;
They were Arizona legends, of that there was no
    doubt.
And once a year they'd go to town when rodeo time
    was near,
And beat the pros on saddle broncs; in Texas they
    had no peer.

I'd tell him 'bout Boots and Wendell Guest* and the
    country that they rode;
It was rougher than any Texas land, and on and on I
    crowed.
I told him that the roughest brush that Texas had
    around
Would be where Boots throwed out his herd and
    called it cuttin' ground.

Ropin', ridin', rollin' rocks—Arizonans wrote the
  book.
Even in country dancin', it'd be first place they took.
My quiet husband 'ud ride along and act like he
  agreed.
I never knew that in his mind brewed a nasty, evil
  deed.

Newlyweds, and still in love, I thought my life a song,
Until one day my husband dear threw his whale line
  on a hog.
We lived along the Brazos on a camp back in the hills,
And ropin' big wild feral hogs was how we got our thrills.

Now those big hogs were runnin' wild and eatin' pecans
  and pear,
And some of them topped 400 pounds, with tushes down
  to there.
They'd pop them teeth and charge your horse and send
  him up a tree,
Unless you had a heeler—with Arizona skills, like me!

Well, my rope came up on just one leg—pigs are short,
  you know—
And my pony wanted shed of him; we was makin' quite
  a show.
To soothe my Arizona pride, these reasons were plenty
  excuse,
And, of course, it was my husband's job to get down and
  turn him loose.

My husband is a dally man, with sixty foot of rope,
But me, I like to tie it on; I thought that I could cope.
When spouse went down to turn him loose, one detail he
  didn't tend:
He left my rope on that hog's one leg, me tied to the other
  end!

He smiled and tipped his hat as he rode off down the draw;
And his final words of encouragement stuck right in my
    craw.
"Maybe, Hon, if your luck is good, and the Lord hears
    what you pray,
Some Arizona cowboy will come ridin' by today."

Somehow I lived through it, 'cause I'm here to tell the tale,
But I promise from that day to this, through every hill
    and dale,
This lady's sung a different song and bragged another
    state;
I found there was no better place than the homeland of
    my mate.

So if you care to argue on where the best are found,
Who ropes the wildest bovines, and where's the roughest
    ground,
Who rides the best cow ponies, or where I'd rather go
    to dances,
I'd have to say with no delay, there ain't *no place like
Texas!*

Bagdad and Mayer towns in Arizona
Ericksons family of good cowboys who have worked on
numerous Arizona ranches
Boots Guest former owner of the Triangle M Ranch at
Mayer, Arizona
Wendell Guest son of Boots

GETTIN' ON

BARNEY NELSON

You cowboys can tell your bronc ride tales
Of fannin' hats and glory,
Of how they spin, sunfish* and dive;
It's all there in your story.

But me, my stories ain't so wild,
I'm just a girl, of course,
And the worst trouble that I seem to have
Is just gettin' on my horse.

I hafta find an old tree stump,
Or a water trough will do,
Creek bank, board fence, salt block,
Walk a mile before I'm through.

And it seems like when I hit a gate
And no high spot within sight,
It's three-strand wire with flimsy posts,
And my pants are awful tight.

Some women claim that cowboys
Don't want them on the crew.
And I guess for boring ladies,
That sure might be true.

But I've never had to beg or plead,
To get to go along,
'Cause their favorite mornin' pastime
Is watching me get on.

---

sunfish a move by a bucking horse where he seems to try
to turn his belly toward the sun

I wrote this one in a creative writing class I was taking at the college. I and some of the highbrows were arguing the merits of cowboy poetry. This was my parting shot. They thought good poetry shouldn't rhyme, so that's why it doesn't—except it almost does, in spite of me.

TIN CUP

BARNEY NELSON

Good wine should slip
    from a crystal glass
Refracting candle light,

But it tastes the same
    from an old tin cup
With one advantage too.

If the wine is bad
    in the crystal glass,
You must assume it's you.

But bad wine served
    in an old tin cup
Just throw the hell away.

SUNDOWN IN THE COW CAMP

JOEL NELSON

The hoodie's washed the dishes
And stacked 'em in the box;
The old cook and the foreman
Have wound and set their clocks.

That horseshoe game they're playin'
Hasta shut down in a while,
'Cause that shadow from the outhouse
Reaches dang near half a mile.

Ol' Charlie's got his guitar out;
That Charlie sure can play.
And it's sundown in the cow camp—
It's my favorite time o' day.

We ate at five this mornin'
'Cept the "Kid"—he skipped his chuck.
He just couldn't eat fer knowin'
That this mornin' horse would buck.

Now the cook has shut the chuck-box lid
And gave the fire a poke,
Throwed some coals around the coffee pot
And lit his evenin' smoke.

His expression kinda clues you
That his memories have flown
To other camps at sundown
And the cowboys that he's known.

The Kid has kept a night horse up;
He's down there in the pens;
Just plumb forgot about his feed;
He's nickerin' fer his friends.

Those calves we worked and turned back out
Have purt'neer mothered up;
Just one cow left a bawlin'.
Think I'll have me one last cup.

You can feel the breeze is shiftin'
Like a cool front's on the way.
Glad the sun's been busy warmin' up
My teepee tent all day.

Some cowboys turn in early—
The cook's the first to go—
While the night owls hug the coffee pot
Till the fire's a dull red glow.

You'll hear it all around the fire—
Poems, politics and song,
Solutions for the price of beef,
Where the BLM went wrong.

That strong and silent cowboy type—
The one you read about—
He's kinda forced to be that way
When the drive's all scattered out.

But he'll get downright eloquent
When the evening chuck's washed down,
And it's sunset in the cow camp,
With the crew gathered 'round.

Half asleep here in my bedroll,
I can hear those night owls laugh;
But that old cow's stopped her bawlin',
So I guess she's found her calf.

THE DRIFTER
AND THE HOMEGUARD

JOEL NELSON

You say you'd like for me to give a detailed
    dissertation
On variations, found by geographical locations,
In the bovine-tending, equine-mounted subspecies of
    man,
Oft endowed unscientifically by moniker of cowhand.

In my opinion unembellished by distracting highbrow
    talk,
They're not really that much different 'cause they all
    sure hate to walk.
Oh, sure, there's lots of difference in the styles of
    gear they use—
These cowboys, these vaqueros, these high-desert
    buckaroos.

But most of them (who really love the life) I think
    you'll find
Shore despise mistreatin' cattle and they'll treat their
    horses kind.
Yet if I had ta group 'em in some general sort of
    way,
There'd be a bunch of them that go and some other
    ones that stay.

He who goes is called the drifter and he never will
  stay put;
He can make it through one wagon work, then gets
  the itchy foot.
He'll winter south and summer north and grubline in
  between,
Just searchin' fer that perfect place where grass is
  always green.

Where the cowboss never yells and where, of course,
  they run a wagon;
Where a feller gets ta rope so much he gets plumb
  tired of draggin';
Where the horses have good withers and can dang
  shore hold a cow;
Where they'd never think of askin' you to weld or
  hay or plow.

Now I'm not knockin' drifters, 'cause they make a
  dang good crew;
They'll ride your snotty horses and they're cowhands
  through and through;
Their campfire talk will mention other ways of
  handlin' cattle;
And they're shore to have some silver and a fancy
  handmade saddle.

Yup, the drifter is the feller that can make the hours
  fly
While the herd is barely movin' and your throat is
  sore and dry.
Still, he's rollin' up and movin' with each changin' of
  the season.
The cow work was a smooth one and the drifters were
  the reason.

He who stays is called a homeguard, and he'll seldom
    ever stray;
He'll keep the outfit runnin'—guess it's always been
    that way.
He'll stay in camp and do those jobs the drifter
    couldn't stand;
And he sits up straight 'n' tall because he's ridin' for
    the brand.

He's startin' colts 'n' scatterin' salt and fixin' water
    gaps;
He's findin' all the trails 'n' such that don't show on
    the maps.
He's pickin' up the remnant, puttin' out the neighbor's
    stray,
And markin' trails with rock piles so the drifters
    know the way.

He's feedin' bulls and makin' sure they're scattered
    in the spring.
Just listen to the hammer make the shoein' anvil ring.
The homeguard knows about what time the cattle go
    to water.
When a cow's had trouble calvin' out, he like as not
    will spot her.

The boss will have him cut the herd and point the
    cattle drive.
At times like this the homeguard is the richest man
    alive.
His string of horses really shines; he's rode 'em all
    their life.
The homeguard's apt to have a damn good cowhand
    for a wife.

I've studied and I've heard it said, as I have asked
    around,
That the homeguard was a drifter 'fore the drifter
    settled down.

THE PRIZE POSSESSION

JOEL NELSON

What's the last thing you would part with?"
I once asked a cowboy pal,
Expecting him to answer,
"Why, that hoss in yon corral."

Or maybe, "That new saddle,"
Which he'd saved for years to git,
Or possibly his granddad's spurs,
Or that silver inlaid bit.

Or the fancy rawhide work
Hangin' in his saddle shed,
Or possibly his roping skill,
Or that pretty girl he'd wed.

A hundred things went through my mind,
From boots to cold, hard cash;
But the thing he promptly answered
Was, "This handlebar mustache!

"Took thirty-five long years, you see,
Ta finally get 'er growed.
And even though it's vain,
I like my old mustachio."

In his ancient quest, Diogenes,*
With lantern in his hand,
Would've found his representative
If he'd stumbled on this man.

And there's hundreds out there like him,
On the western cattle range,
Who cultivate their facial hair
And ain't about to change.

Now the dang things are a nuisance
When winter time moves in,
And you've got two big, long chunks of ice
Hangin' way down past your chin.

And in a while your cold red nose
Will start to run and dribble,
And before you get your mittens off,
That freezes in the middle.

Boy, your napkin gets a workout
When the menu's soup or stew,
And it sometimes gets discolored
From tobacco if you chew.

There's the slow recovery period
When she's singed by brandin' fire,
Or when wife with maddened viselike grip
Should demonstrate her ire.

Or you're maybe shoeing horses,
And this bronc sets up a clamor,
And a handlebar gets hung twixt claws
On the downstroke of your hammer.

There's the, "Ooh, that tickles, Honey,"
When the ends get nice and long,
And you have to readapt your style
Of talkin' on the phone.

Oh, the trials and tribulations
Of the man with the mustache
Are just the dues he has to pay
To possess a bit more dash.

To receive those looks of wonder and awe
From the kids with peach-fuzz lip,
And the fascinated looks from babes
Who reach and grab ahold of it.

But they say it's really worth it,
And you feel that you've come far
When you see that dashing buckaroo
In the mirror behind the bar.

Oh, sure, you'll hear some whispers,
And those out of range make cracks.
But just straighten up, take out the tube,
And add a little wax!

Diogenes Greek philosopher of the school that believed vir-
tue was the only good and that its essence lay in self-control
and independence

GOOD, CLEAN FUN!

ROD NELSON

I remember making hay with Dad,
   we'd put it up in stacks—
Dad used to use a stack frame
   and fill it to the max.

Then sometimes, but not often,
   he'd say, "Rodney, you've the knack—
Grab a fork—I'll lift you up,
   and you top off the stack.

Reluctantly, I'd take the fork;
   he'd lift me up on top.
I'd stack that hay to thirty feet
   before he'd finally stop.

Then he'd drive up really close;
   I could see him down beneath,
As I stepped out on the pushoff
   on the end of the stacker teeth.

He'd back up a little ways;
   I hoped he'd try no tricks,
But giving me rides on that farmhand
   was how he got his kicks!

Wasn't long and I'd get mad,
   I'd had these rides before:
He'd slide the pushoff almost in,
   then he'd run it out once more.

"Come on, Dad, let me down;
   this really isn't fair."
Then he'd point the teeth toward the ground,
   and leave me dangling in the air!

I could hear him laughing down below,
  in hopeless, choking mirth,
And I'd wonder if I'd ever again
  have my feet upon the earth!

It was no use to argue.
  Dad wouldn't quit 'til he was done.
But I always, *always* wondered
  how could this be so fun?!

Well, our yard light burned out last year,
  and since I'd run that farmhand all my life,
I knew we could fix it in a minute,
  if I could convince the wife!

Wasn't easy to convince her;
  she said a housewife was her role.
Though mad she was, she climbed aboard,
  took a ride to the top of the pole.

I said, "Sweetheart, I'm so proud of you,"
  when she had fixed the light.
"And you're 'specially lovely when you're angry;
  you really are a sight!"

"Let me down, you worthless cur,"
  she was having a full-fledged fit.
I couldn't pass up a chance like this,
  so I drove around a bit!

Good, clean fun, I said to myself
  as she called me a hopeless sap.
My grin got even wider
  as I made another lap!

"Honey, just enjoy yourself;
  and isn't it a fright—
It's the first time that I've carried you
  since our wedding night!"

I finally shut the tractor off,
  let her sit up there a while,

Promised her I'd let her down,
    if she would only smile.

Oh, it was fun—but there's a problem,
    I can see it now, I can:
It's gonna take some mighty sweet talkin'
    when that light burns out again!

A 2:00 A.M. CALL

ROD NELSON

A 2:00 A.M. call is no fun at all
    For a rancher who needs his rest.
"To heck with that thing—just let it ring."
    Bud wouldn't leave his warm nest.

"But, Bud," Liz cried, "maybe someone has died."
    Her voice, though uncertain, was warning.
"Well, Liz," Bud said, "if anyone's dead,
    They'll still be dead in the morning!"

THE SALMON RIVER BREAKS

HOWARD L. NORSKOG

There are days of sun and sand and stone,
Where me and my lady stayed alone.
We lived our days
In the misty haze,
Where the bighorn sheep came down to graze
In the Salmon River Breaks.*

We built a home of strong pine log,
And our only friend was a yellow dog.
We splashed like fools
In the water cool,
Where the great outdoors was the only school,
In the Salmon River Breaks.

I trapped the beaver and sold his skin.
She cursed this place that we lived in
And dreamed of spice
And houses nice;
We even left this hell hole twice,
In the Salmon River Breaks.

But me and the lady, we returned;
There was something within our souls that burned;
For the stars at night
Are a beautiful sight,
Where the grizzly and panther sometimes fight,
In the Salmon River Breaks.

I swear we could tell you a thousand tales,
Where we lived by the side of the Nez Perce Trail,
And the deer come down
With scarce a sound,
Where the elk and the mountain goat abound
In the Salmon River Breaks.

The River of No Return flows free,
And winter and summer seem to be
A part of the strife
That infects my life;
And I thank the Lord for a loving wife,
In the Salmon River Breaks.

For they say back there in times gone past,
That the Master decided this land should last,
And the ones inane
Couldn't play their games;
So this beautiful place would remain the same
In the Salmon River Breaks.

So the truth of it is, I love it here,
And that's why I stay year after year.
And on a sunny day You can lay me away
Where the eagle and osprey come to play—
In the Salmon River Breaks.

Salmon River Breaks just south of the Nez Perce Trail
in northern Idaho

TAKERS

HOWARD L. NORSKOG

The government took all his horses,
And the bank hauled his cattle away.
It seems that the hay he stacked against winter
Caught fire and burned several days.

They told him the land was going for forfeit
To pay some back taxes come due.
The chickens they planned on for groceries
Were molting; and he had the flu.

The pickup was now out of gas that would help
To get him the job he would need;
So the order said, "Vacate the premises now,
If you cannot pay up with all speed!

We're coming to take everything that you have.
Your credit's no good, so we've found.
And the only thing that you have left now of value,
Strange as it seems, is the ground."

But he had him a rifle and twenty-odd shells,
And he sets on the porch by the door;
For he has decided that, oddly enough,
They ain't going to take anymore.

So he left them a note over there by the door,
Near the top, on the side of the jamb,
And it said, "You are coming to get me,
But, frankly, I don't give a damn.

"My great-grandfather settled this place;
His grave's on top of the hill.
And my grandpa and grandma still share a spot
On that knoll where the breezes blow still.

"My mother and father rest there beside them,
Where some dogs and some kittens reside.
The history that strings out behind us,
All rest on that hill side by side.

"You tell me you're bringing the National Guard,
And the sheriff's office sent every man.
Why, you even conscribed some civilians—
You must have a hell of a plan

"To do in this cowboy who sets on the porch,
And whiles his last hours away,
I never did dream I could be so important,
Just when I leave you today."

The soldiers in battle dress came through the trees,
And the other men came by the wall.
He watched as they came, then raised up his rifle;
But he never fired at all.

The rifles spit fire and he fell to the ground,
And everyone bragged how they'd done.
They talked like a game they were playing,
And some even seemed to have fun.

And when they all walked by the body there lying,
The note once again could be seen—
The one near the top of the door jamb—
And it caused one or two to turn green.

It said...

"My great-grandfather settled this place;
His grave's on top of the hill.
And my grandpa and grandma share a spot
On that knoll where the breezes blow still.

"My mother and father rest there beside them,
Where some dogs and some kittens reside.
The history that streams out behind us,
All rest on that hill side by side.

"So bury me up with the others,
With my family and the ones who have cared.
I've willed all this place to the takers;
I've given this land we have shared.

"Tell everyone that you came with your people
To kill one old cowboy alone,
That you heroically shot him down laughing,
And how he's at last traveled home."

THE BLACK LADY MARE

HOWARD L. NORSKOG

There's a colt that's following my Black Lady mare,
Down there just south of the house;
He's kind of a light-colored tan or a brown,
So maybe I'll just call him the Mouse.

Old Black Lady's kicked me a dozen times,
And lately she's bitten me twice;
She's stepped on my foot and broken three toes,
So I'm not considering she's nice.

She's so mean that we muzzle the son of a gun
And tie up four feet when she's shoed.
She's bucked till I threw up my dinner all over—
There wasn't much else I could do.

She's bucked off my brother and the hired hand,
And left them all skinned up and sore,
Till we got to hating the day she was born,
And none of us ride her no more.

But one thing for sure: she throws a hell of a colt,
And that's all that keeps her alive—
Though for a four-bit piece and a broken bit,
I swear that mare would die.

But just when I think it, I look out the window,
And I'm king of all I survey,
Including that ugly old Black Lady horse
Who's waiting to get me today.

But out in the badlands, in a blizzard last Christmas,
I was lost, all give out and froze.
My pony had run off and left me alone,
And icicles hung from my nose.

There was no place to hide from the treacherous
   wind,
And not one thin chance to survive.
When those people who cared came out in the
   morning,
They just wouldn't find me alive.

But out of the storm came that Black Lady pony;
I could swear she was wearing a grin.
So I grabbed at her tail and followed her there,
And, sure enough, she brought me in.

So I forgave all the things that the old horse had
   done
And proclaimed her great praises to all;
In flowery phrases I conjured up pictures
To make sure her image can't fall.

So if this is true, I'm sure that you wonder
Why I'm wearing this cast on my shin.
Well, just when I'm thinking I figured her out,
That old biddy kicked me again.

GOING TO TOWN FOR PARTS

GWEN PETERSEN

Whenever the tractor quits or balks
Or the mower refuses to start,
I'm the one my husband talks
Into going to town for parts.

No matter I'm buried clear up to my eyes
In bread dough and Pillsbury flour,
I dust off my hands, out the door I fly,
Vowing return in an hour.

While my knight of the tractor comforts his steed,
In the pickup I roar into town,
A good woman off on an errand of need
To the store where parts can be found.

A part man's a smart man who knows all factors
Of flange and bolt and U-joint,
For healing the wounds of old broken tractors;
He patiently waits as I point.

"That left-handed flange with a gasket and hose,"
I say with confident air;
With a withering glance down his Cyrano nose
He asks, "Just one or a pair?"

Confusion wells up and I know I'm pathetic,
"Oh, both," nonchalantly I say;
Twenty miles to drive home; my life is hectic,
I've lost the best of the day.

Back at the ranch, I seek out my husband;
"Look, one of each," I declaim.
He takes the flange with an eager hand,
Then utters a tasteless name.

"A flange is no good without some bolts,"
He growls with amazed disdain,
"Anyone could see, even fools and dolts!"
My ego begins to wane.

Three trips to town and one flat tire,
And what do I find in the end?
The tractor gets fixed with pliers and wire—
No wonder I'm round the bend!

WOMAN OF THE LAND

GWEN PETERSEN

Her name won't be in history books,
This woman of the land;
Her heart is where it wants to be,
Content with Heaven's plan.

And in the corridors of time,
Her way is counted true;
Enduring hardships, strong as rock,
She does what she must do.

Born when wire had begun
To stitch up prairie seams,
When homesteads patched the western land—
Quilts of hope-filled dreams.

A herder's wagon was her home
In sun or rain or wind;
She and Pa did outside work,
While Sis and Ma stayed in.

Her pa hired out his greyhound dogs
To track the coyotes down;
With hounds in cages, he would drive
From ranch to farm to town.

Pa never settled down for long,
For when the bounty slowed,
They packed the wagons, hitched the teams,
And traveled down the road.

Sometimes Pa would trade for goods
Like shoes for her or Sis;
And once he got a violin,
Its song was like a kiss.

But Pa resold the fiddle for
Another purebred hound.
She watched it go without a word
And cried without a sound.

They lived a while at Carlo's house,
The Flathead tribal chief;
A gentle man and kind, she says,
Who never showed his grief.

In hand-me-downs she walked for miles
To learn to read and write;
For school was just a sometime thing,
Wherever Pa would light.

But when she reached her sixteenth year,
She caught a cowboy's eye;
He asked her would she marry him
And make him apple pie.

As partner, double-harnessed now,
She worked beside her man;
They saved and bought a modest spread
And settled on their land.

She toiled in cold and snow and wet,
Or heat that scorched her bones;
No 'lectric lights to chase the dark,
No plumbing in their home.

She saw the land was good and strong
And planned to run some sheep;
And when he called her fool, she said,
"These woollies I will keep."

They cared for cattle side by side,
Though sheep were hers alone;
But in the fall, the lamb checks paid
The interest on the loan.

Then Nature dealt another hand—
A child was due in May;
And though it didn't slow her much,
She did take off one day.

The baby boy was strong until
Pneumonia won the fight;
The child was buried on their land;
She battled grief at night.

Then trailing cows, her pony fell
In crashing, crushing pile;
Her belly took the saddle horn,
And town was thirty mile.

Her cowboy found her, took her in;
To God he made a plea.
They patched her up, her scars grew dim,
But children weren't to be.

She poured her spirit into work
On land that gave—and took;
She held no grudge and never cast
A single backward look.

As years slipped by in River Time,
Her cowboy lost his sight.
They sold the ranch and bought a place
More suited to his plight.

One day he started 'cross the road,
She shouted—caught her breath!
Her cowboy never saw the car
That dashed him to his death.

And now she ran the ranch alone;
And with her partner gone,
The only thing remaining true—
The land was there each dawn.

As time and strength began to wane,
She took another chance
And bought a tiny piece of earth—
A widow woman's ranch.

There's sheep and rabbits, goats for milk,
And hens for eggs or stew.
She doesn't wait for other folks
To tell her what to do.

She's planted trees to shade the house
And sowed some grass for hay;
She irrigates her rocky patch,
Stays busy through the day.

Her hands are gnarled, her step is slow,
Yet when she's asked to town
By kindly Senior Center folks,
She always turns them down.

"I haven't time, I've chores," she says;
"They're what I aim to do;
My heart is where it wants to be;
My land will see me through."

Though her name won't be in history books,
And her range is less than grand,
Her heart is where it wants to be—
This woman of the land.

LIMERICKS

GWEN PETERSEN

For riding way out on the prairie,
The facilities tend to be airy;
    You can bet from the spot
    Where you've chosen to squat,
That your profile will show—so don't tarry.

————

Though little in life is for sure,
Three things on the ranch will endure—
    Sticky mud to your thighs,
    Ugly bugs every size,
And a steady supply of manure.

————

A cowboy hat's made with great pains
To guard him from sunshine and rains,
    With a wide band for sweat
    So his eyes don't get wet,
And a crown that's too big for his brains.

————

Cowboys get up before dawn,
With many a curse and a yawn;
They eat plumb half-hearted, And wait to get started
    A day they now claim is half gone.

A WORKING RANCH

GWEN PETERSEN

We envy you," said my city friends,
"Your life in the great outdoors.
We're thinking of buying a ranch somewhere
And living a life like yours.

"We'll have a garden—our very own,
And keep lots of animals there;
A working ranch," they said—and smiled,
And their eyes held a faraway stare.

In my ears I can hear their words ring plain
As I start on my morning chore;
With two heavy buckets of water and grain
I head for the chicken house door.

As I enter the scabby, unpainted shed
To a roomful of clucking hens,
I see the gazebo with white wicker chairs
On the lawn of my city friends.

I picture them tossing sunflower seeds
To a twittering songbird band.
Then a setting hen ends my reverie
By pecking a hole in my hand.

I leave with my bucket of fresh-laid eggs
And step in a juicy cowpie;
My feet do the splits—I crash in the dirt
And the eggs fly off for the sky.

As I lie supine, I spy from the ground
That the garden gate is awry,
And there six heifers are munching around
In my summer food supply.

My two frantic collies and I commence
To bark and scream and yell;
The heifers depart by way of the fence,
Trampling it all to—well.

I fix the fence and enter the house
As a neighbor phones to say
That my horses have wandered into his field
And are eating his prime cut hay.

And do I want my registered saddle mare bred
To his workhorse stud, asks he.
"No, no!" I screech, and filled with dread,
I move with alacrity.

My city friends wear designer jeans;
My city friends eat quiche;
They have a courtyard full of flowers
And poodles trained to the leash.

But they yearn for a working ranch, they claim,
To experience its joys and its fun.
Another day like this has been
And, hell—I'll give 'em this one.

GENERATIONS

VESS QUINLAN

More than casual
But less than
Constant companions...
Friends,
Like our fathers
Before us.

A chance meeting,
Last met
At my father's funeral.
And of his father?
"Hadn't I heard?
Dead in December."
"Sorry."

We talk then
About the old men;
Of teasing
The black bull
With his dad's
New pickup,
Until
The beast pawed dirt
At the very sound
of a V8 engine;
How his dad,
Ignorant of the game
And with a caved-in door,
Always wondered
What in hell
Got into that damn bull.

We laugh sadly,
Knowing
His father's death
Makes us
The old men now.

THE BARN CATS

VESS QUINLAN

It's funny, the things you remember;
Like accepting without question
That it was your solemn duty
To study hard and earn big money
Because parents suffered the depression.

How on your tenth birthday
You walked down to milk
With a staggering headache,
Sat on the one-legged stool
And pressed your forehead
Against her silken flank.

How you remember dull ringing sounds
As the first squirts hit bottom;
How the sound changed to a quiet hiss
As foaming milk filled the shiny bucket;
How the smell of fresh warm milk
Rose to mingle with the clean-cow smell;
How the barn cats sat half-circled,
Mewing politely, insisting there was enough
To fill their little pan.

How the gentle cow responded
To strong brown hands
And let down her milk;
How calmness and forbearance
Were transmitted through your skull;
How your pain was drawn
Into the patient cow.

And now, years later,
You stare out a city window
And ask yourself if big money
Is really better than barn cats
And cow-cured headaches.

PASSING THE MANTLE

VESS QUINLAN

How small he was
And how he struggled
With the work;
He irrigated, fed, doctored,
And learned, as I had,
The difference between
Right and close,
Then sought my approval
To validate his knowing.

How strange it seems,
And how right,
That a simple passage
Of time has brought
Us here where I finish
This day of favorite work
And look to my son
For his approval.

THE OLD HANDS

VESS QUINLAN

It's good to set and listen
To their talk of long ago,
These men with skin like leather
And hair as white as snow,

To hear how the world was run
A little different then,
Produced a tougher breed of cattle
And a rougher sort of men.

The cows were lean and ringy*
And working 'em was hard;
You could melt a hundred head
And not get a pound of lard.

There were damn few gentle horses
Like we're used to now;
It don't take much to figger horses
Had to match with man and cow.

A horse was five or six years old
Before they'd run him in;
The idea of starting colts
Was considered wrong back then.

Their days were long and lonesome
And the camps were far away;
They got to town about once a month
To spend the hard-earned pay.

But the thing you hear most often
Is the whole damn deal was fun,
In spite of winter's biting cold
And summer's scorching sun,

In spite of rank and spoiled horses,
Or maybe 'cause of them.
You wonder if you'd have made a hand
Had you lived back then.

You say you wish the old days
Would come rolling back around,
To see who'd stay the camp
And who'd go back to town.

A gray head shakes,"No, son," he says,
"Not that, leastways not to the letter.
We done some things the way we did
'Cause we just didn't know no better."

ringy wild and spooky, referring to cattle

SOLD OUT

VESS QUINLAN

The worst will come tomorrow
When we load the saddle horses.
We are past turning back;
The horses must be sold.

The old man turns away, hurting,
As the last cow is loaded.
I hunt words to ease his pain
But there is nothing to say.

He walks away to lean
On a top rail of the corral
And look across the calving pasture
Toward the willow-grown creek.

I follow,
Absently mimicking his walk,
And stand a post away.
We don't speak of causes or reasons,

Don't speak at all;
We just stand there
Leaning on the weathered poles,
While shadows consume the pasture.

ANTHEM

BUCK RAMSEY

And in the morning I was riding
Out in the breaks of that long plain,
And leather creaking in the quieting
Would sound with trot and trot again.
I lived in time with horse hoof falling;
I listened well and heard the calling
The earth, my mother, bade to me,
Though I would still ride wild and free.
And as I flew out on the morning
Before the bird, before the dawn,
I was the poem, I was the song.
My heart would beat the world a warning—
Those horsemen now rode all with me,
And we were good and we were free.

We were not told, but ours the knowing
We were the native strangers there
Among the things of prairie growing—
This knowing gave us more the care
To let the grass keep at its growing
And let the streams keep at their flowing.
We knew the land would not be ours,
That no one has the awful powers
To claim the vast and common nesting,
To own the life that gave him birth,
Much less to rape his Mother Earth
And ask her for a mother's blessing,
And ever live in peace with her,
And, dying, come to rest with her.

Oh, we would ride and we would listen
And hear the message on the wind.
The grass in morning dew would glisten
Until the sun would dry and blend
The grass to ground and air to skying.
We'd know by bird or insect flying,
Or by their mood or by their song,
If time and moon were right or wrong
For fitting works and rounds to weather.
The critter coats and leaves of trees
Might flash some signal with a breeze—
Or wind and sun on flow'r or feather.
We knew our way from dawn to dawn,
And far beyond, and far beyond.

It was the old ones with me riding
Out through the fog fall of the dawn,
And they would press me to deciding
If we were right or we were wrong.
For time came we were punching cattle
For men who knew not spur nor saddle,
Who came with locusts in their purse
To scatter loose upon the earth.
The savage had not found this prairie
Till some who hired us came this way
To make the grasses pay and pay
For some raw greed no wise and wary
Regard for grass could satisfy.
The old ones wept, and so did I.

Do you remember? We'd come jogging
To town with jingle in our jeans,
And in the wild night we'd be bogging
Up to our hats in last month's dreams.
It seemed the night could barely hold
With all those spirits to embold us
While, horses waiting on three legs,

We'd drain the night down to the dregs.
And just before beyond redemption
We'd gather back to what we were,
We'd leave the money left us there
And head our horses for the wagon.
But in the ruckus, in the whirl
We were the wolves of all the world.

The grass was growing scarce for grazing,
Would soon turn sod or soon turn bare.
The money men set to replacing
The good and true in spirit there.
We could not say, there was no knowing,
How ill the future winds were blowing.
Some cowboys even shunned the ways
Of cowboys in the trail-herd days,
(But where's the gift not turned for plunder?)
Forgot that we are what we do
And not the stuff we lay claim to.
I dream the spell that we were under—
I throw in with a cowboy band
And go out horseback through the land.

So mornings now I'll go out riding
Through pastures of my solemn plain,
And leather creaking in the quieting
Will sound with trot and trot again.
I'll live in time with horse hoof falling,
I'll listen well and hear the calling
The earth, my mother, bids to me,
Though I will still ride wild and free.
And as I fly out on the morning
Before the bird, before the dawn,
I'll be this poem, I'll be this song.
My heart will beat the world a warning—
Those horsemen will ride all with me,
And we'll be good, and we'll be free.

THE CHRISTMAS WALTZ

BUCK RAMSEY

The winter is here and the old year is passing,
The sun in its circle winds far in the south.
It's time to bring cheer to a cold snowbound cow
    camp,
It's Christmas tree time of the year for the house.

Go ride to the cedar break rim of a canyon,
Down by where the river takes creek water clear,
And saddle-sleigh home us a fine shapely evergreen
Picked out while prowling the pastures this year.

While Fair strings the berries and popcorn and
    whatnots
And Kid braids the wreaths out of leather and vines,
Old Dunder, he whittles and whistles old carols
And fills them with stories of fine olden times.

He talks of a baby boy born in a cow shed,
All swaddled in tatters and laid in a trough,
Who, growing up, gave away all he could gather
And taught us that what is not given is lost.

It's morning of Christmas and long before dawning
The camp hands are risen to ready the feast.
But with the fires glowing they don warm apparel
And go out to gaze on the Star of the East.

They cobbler the plums they put up back in summer,
They bake a wild turkey and roast backstrap deer,
They dollop the sourdough for rising and baking,
And pass each to each now the brown jug of cheer.

The dinner is done and they pass out the presents.
Their three each they open with handshakes and
    hugs,
Then Kid gets his guitar and Fred gets his fiddle
While Dunder and Fair laugh and roll back the rugs.

The tunes that they play melt the chill from the
    winter
As Dunder and Fair waltz and two-step along.
They play, sing and dance till the next morning's
    dawning,
Then all of their slumbers are filled with this song.

COWBOY WENT A-COURTIN'

BUCK RAMSEY

This bunkhouse talk of cowboy romance
Left other whirls in second place:
Poor Dobbin Brown sat all in silence
When Yucca Spear strung out the ways
Old Dobbin choused the Widow Horton,
A proper lady he went courtin'
Down out of Denton in those days
They built trail herds for Ira Hayes.
He'd slicked his hair with warm hog taller
And sloshed up good with blossom juice
And then asked Yucca what good ruse
To ply her with that would allow her
To see him with the kind of eyes
That shaped him up about her size.

"Just tell her," Yucca said, "you're earnin'
Your wages horseback punchin' cows.
There's nary woman live not yearnin'
To take in all the law allows
Of us young princes of the prairie—
Though some might tell it quite contrary.
You've got to make her think that you'd
Pulled feats that only top hands could.
Just tell her of your fancy ropin'
When we were skinnin' dead cows out,
Describe in detail all about
You shakin' out your twine and lopin'
To loop that buzzard—how it left
It's mornin' grazin's on your vest."

When Yucca gave him this instruction
He said ol' Dobbin swelled with pride,
Commenced to couch the tale in fustian
Detail and prose that would have vied
With Shakespeare Jones, the big black cookie
Who did Othello for the lucky
Cowhands camped with his wagon band
When Melpomene took his hand.
The widow set her finest table.
From soup to fluff duff it was more
Than he had ever seen before.
It was far more than she was able
To set before him at one time.
He sloshed it down with her plum wine.

Her tablecloth of lace, her china,
Clean white with blueprint curlicues—
Ol' Dobbin never saw it finer
Until it came his time to choose
The bowls from which to ladle helpings.
The cones of silver mesh had kept them
From all attraction to the fare
Until the hog fat on his hair
Invited house flies to his dinner.
They made a halo 'round his head.
"It's right fine vittles," Dobbin said.
Such eloquence, he thought, might win her
Intrigue and keep her feelings warm
Till he could ply her with his charm.

But here's the tale as told by Yucca:
"So there he sat, his hat of flies
Upon his head as she served supper.
On top of that, the widow was,
You might say, discombobulated—
That does mean, don't it, agitated?
Concerned about her tableware,
For she quite simply didn't care
For Dobbin's manner with her dishes.
The way he ate, she was afraid
He'd take a bite of plate instead.
I tell you, if her looks and wishes
Could turn into an absent pill
He'd be long gone with half a meal.

"But hints and looks don't take with Dobbin.
Through eatin', he sinks in a chair
And spurs her rug and goes to jobbin'
A big cigar 'round in the air
Till pore Miz Horton brings a candle.
He settles back and takes a handle, Sorts out his
     thoughts, then cranks up to
Begin the tale I told to you:
'I 'uz skinnin' dead cows out that summer
And flat out roped a carr'on bird—
A feat you've likely never heard.
Of course, I never figgered on 'er
Upchuckin' dinner on my vest, . . .'
That's when he heard her last request."

THE NEW KID IS OUTFITTED

BUCK RAMSEY

They decked him down with boots and leggings,
They decked him up with vest and hat,
They geared him out with all the riggings
A cowboy needs to make his tack.
The cantle curved high on his saddle,
The horn was anchored to hold cattle
On his riata of rawhide,
The swells were for the pitching ride.
His bridle of remuda colors—
The gray, the sorrel, bay and black—
Were from the fancy braided tack
Of one of sundry other fellers
Who'd come to join a cowboy band
And failed to ever make a hand.

The boots and leggings had been Charlie's;
He'd wandered west from Arkansas.
The vest and hat were Jingle Farley's;
He'd gone back home to see his ma
And, like so many 'nother youngun
Who couldn't hack what had to be done,
Left every cowboy thing behind,
Discarded all that might remind
Him of the days out on the prairie.
The saddle was Black Jim's; he froze
In one bad winter's blowing snows.
His rope had hung Red Poison Berry.
Some braided reins had once been Ed's;
He thirsted out of broken legs.

TO A COWBOY'S GRANDSON

GENE RANDELS

A late spring blizzard
delivered me
To a snug sod house
on the Arikaree.*

As my world
slowly grew
To dooryard size—
awesome, huge!

At twilight in the
evenin' still,
I heard a turtledove
and a whippoorwill,

Until a spotted pony
set me free
To ride the Black Wolf,*
Dry Willow* and Arikaree.

There I felt
the scorching sun,
Saw killing drought
in thirty-one,

Saw the tornado's
awful wrath,
Fled terrified
from its warpath.

My father grazed
Hereford cattle here
With badger, hawk
and mule-eared deer.

In a dry wash
I found arrowhead
Of nomad warriors
long since dead.

I found an unglazed
pot one day,
With strange designs
pressed in the clay.

When I raised it
from the sand
I think I touched
the potter's hand.

In a buffalo wallow
fairy ring
I sometimes sat and dreamed
strange dreams.

In the grass I saw
a yellow gleam,
Large rifle shells,
very old and green.

But can it survive
the dreadful hand
Of the destroyer God
called modern man?

On a lonely,
forgotten, wartime hill,
The night became
a shot-torn hell.

I drew back deep
within the core of me;
I found the Black Wolf,
Dry Willow and Arikaree.

Now, I don't crave
exotic shores;
I look fondly back
to youth once more.

If you reveal
your special place,
Go, when Winter slacks
its cold embrace,

When Spring's soft rains
recharge the sand
And wildflowers blanket
the greening land.

Then the picture the mind
holds and loves
Is the very best
it ever was.

My grandson rode
today with me
Over the Black Wolf,
Dry Willow and Arikaree.

He talked of troubled schools,
of children's hate,
Of atomic bombs,
the doomed world's fate.

A child wasn't asked,
in nature's plan,
To face the fears
of full-grown man.

Too young for the world
we've brought about,
Besieged within,
assailed without.

Let him grow his roots
into the land,
Then foursquare, rooted,
he can stand.

Let him dream the dreams
that I once knew,
Of Samarkand
and Xanadu,

Why would a hunter leave
shells lie here,
When to a hunter
brass was dear?

Then on the hill
I saw a buffalo skull;
I heard the rifle fire,
saw the buffalo fall.

A silent gun
in a vanished hand,
At a long-forgotten
hunter's stand.

Or did the hunter
perish too,
By Cheyenne lance—
or was it Sioux?

I saw painted warriors
against the sky,
Their feathered heads
held proud and high.

On spotted ponies
they swept by,
Thundering hooves,
fierce battle cry.

A war club raised,
the hunter fell,
Then they vanished;
it was deathly still.

Then I dreamed
of larger things
Than arrowheads
and fairy rings.

I read a book;
I saw afar;
My mind soared out
to a new guide star.

With feet deep rooted
in this land,
I stormed the walls
of Samarkand.*

I took Coromandel
and Mandalay,*
Walked the crooked wall
of old Cathay.*

As youthful dreams
fade one by one,
Reality blocks the Dreamer's sun.

I watched an eagle
high ... afar,
Fold wings and fall
like a burning star.

The squeal of eaglet food
drifted back to me,
For a bird of prey's
posterity.

It's written here
with fang and claw:
The strong shall rise,
the weak shall fall.

This my enchanted,
much-loved land,
War, drought, famine,
it can withstand.

See the geese cross the moon
in a lowering sky,
Feel his heart respond
to the wanderer's cry,

Feed a bucket calf,
watch an eagle fly,
See spotted fawns,
hear a coyote's cry.

I'll teach him many important things—
Of willow whistles,
of fairy rings;

Tell him of the morning star
and great steam trains;
Of a riverman
we called Mark Twain;

Tell him of Lindy's
lonely flight;
Of a steam train's whistle
on a frosty night;

Let him glory in life
to his fingertips
Before he dreads the bomb
and makes micro-chips.

Then he can look in the face
of any man
And say, "This I think,
and this I am!"

And when the world
has wrung you out,
Taught you fear
and how to doubt,

Look deep inside
your heart, to me;
We'll ride the Black Wolf,
Dry Willow and Arikaree.

Arikaree and Dry Willow creeks in northeastern
Colorado
Black Wolf spirit protector, as in Indian lore, for the
Randels family
Samarkand Alexander the Great destroyed the city of
Samarkand in 329 B.C.
Mandelay second-largest city of Burma, captured by
British in 1885
Cathay Marco Polo called China *Cathay* in his accounts of
his travels to the land of Kublai Khan

THE NEW HAND

GENE RANDELS

He gets all the spoiled horses,
The bed far from the fire,
The seat far down the table;
He gets to string all the "bob-wire."

The cowboss glares at him
Like a Hereford bull at an Angus calf;
He feels all knuckles and elbows;
He can't seem to show any class.

He feels low as a sheepherder's mama,
Like a calf that's lost from his ma;
He's thinkin' of rollin' his bedroll;
His pride's been rubbed bleedin' raw—

Until a Triple C cowpuncher
Started crowdin' the boy at the bar.
The cowboss said, "Hey, ugly booger,
Don't push that boy too far.

"Or mebbe you're wantin' some of my action.
I'll see that you're bedded in flowers.
Why, you'd rather lock horns with the devil!
That cowboy, he's one of ours."

TOP HAND

GENE RANDELS

I've rode the high side
Since the day I was born.
If you crowd the bull,
You're gonna take the horn.

I got a scrap-iron face
On a cast-iron frame;
Bullets bounce off of me
And I rust when it rains.

You half-bad dudes
Walk wide around me,
Unless you just can't wait
To see eternity.

I'm a wheelhorse*
And a workin' fool;
In the oil fields
I push the tool.

In the mines I'm known
As the walkin' dog;
In Dixie they call me
The old tusk hawg.*

I ain't no bad man;
Don't push no man around;
I'm not bad to know—
I just don't give no ground.

I can be found
All across this land,
Where men hit life hard
And gotta be top hand.

wheelhorse the horse in a hitched team that controls all
movements of the team
tusk hawg a javelina—wild boar with tusks

---

*The rich Europeans who came out into the American West a
hundred years ago were younger sons of titled or monied families.
They came to get rich on their own terms. Where they came from,
they spent a great deal of time and money keeping the working
class humble. The western people they met had over a hundred
years to get over being humble. As a matter of fact, if they had
been humble, they wouldn't have come west to start with.*

THE SHORTHORN
GENE RANDELS

Rupert Walpole, late of London,
Thought he'd do well out West,
For he had various muscles
And some hair upon his chest.

He wore a half a pair of glasses,
Had a turkey-struttin' walk,
A rank and ugly manner,
And a mean-mouthed way to talk.

I hired on to run his pack string.
You oughta see the gear he brung;
After two days on the job,
I knew he'd likely cash in young.

He got as far as Ogallala,
Where he talked a cowboy down,
Till he grabbed Rupert by his guzzlum
And he turned his damper down.

In Laramie lived Grizzly Nelson;
He was a nasty piece of work.
I'll never know why Rupert
Had to give his rope a jerk.

But Nelson, he stood hip shot,
Just as if he didn't hear,
Till he gathered up old Rupert's slack
And bit the dewlap off his ear.

He stayed quiet clear to Reno,
Where he met Texas Slim.
Ya know, I think old Rupert's light
Was mebbe just a little dim.

Now Slim didn't come to Reno
In search of fame or wealth;
He outrun a Texas posse,
So it was mostly for his health.

Rupert leaned his mean on Texas Slim
And the crowd was filled with awe;
Why, you could've heard a pin drop
When them shooters come to taw.

I'm here to testify
That Texan's gun was quick.
He blew Rupert's light out
And then he trimmed his wick.

So Rupert got his empire
Out in the western land.
It measured about six by three
In Boot Hill desert sand.

TAIL THAT'S LIGHT

HENRY REALBIRD

Goin' on fresh snow,
Snow's been fallin'
Several days,
The ground, all is white,
Sagebrush tops
Stickin' out of snow;
Ridin' through snow, it's quiet,
River where it goes.
Just the trees are black,
The ground, all is white;
Where there are pine trees
It's sorta blue, almost black
Still farther beyond
Wolf Teeth Mountains, pine trees are blue,
There's nothing but the cold wind
Look sorta like smoke;
Ash trees, where they're thick
It is black.
Gray I'm ridin',
His breath is white,
Gray ... ground he is like this day.
My song, I'm singin'
Lookin' around
Where the sun appears
Pink, peeps out of blue sky;
Goin' to get many horses
Ridin' gray, they won't see me
In white gray, blue black winter day;
My song, I'm singin'.

AMONG SHOOTIN' STARS

HENRY REALBIRD

Sold bronc saddle,
Foreclosed cows
Through the broken pieces
Of shattered dreams.
The dreamer wrote this
From the hollowed feeling of a cloud
Above Thompson Creek
In the Wolf Teeth Mountains,*
When he used to dream
On the road to California
As he watched
The ground turn to mud
From under the chuck wagon fly
As he sat on the tongue
Jingling spur rowels,
A howl in coyote cry
Lurkin' in shadows
Left in time—
Such is the feeling that I'm

Head over heels in love with the stars,
Feeling in the hills among the shootin' stars,
Stuck in the rhythm of a northbound freight
To the buffalo jump bars
In the streets and the cars,
For just a thumb to catch a ride that's late
I rode on through the gate.

Met up with a feeling
Lost on the road,
Wild horse camp feeling
Shoulda been told

Before this ever was
Pictures of feeling
Stuck in time,
Inscription on buckles,
Twinkle on chime,
Broncs and women, to glass of wine
Brought back by chuckles
Only to hawk the buckles.
The truth
Is what you know
As to be true
Underneath the snow,
Not what you think
As to be true
In sky turn blue.

Head over heels in love with the stars,
Feeling in the hills among the shootin' stars,
Stuck in the rhythm of a northbound freight
To the buffalo jump bars In the streets and the cars,
For just a thumb to catch a ride that's late
I rode on through the gate.

The return to cowboy wages
Turn back the pages
Thought from where wildflowers grow
And peaceful fires glow
Around teepee rings,
Sweet smell of sage
Among the pine
From out the grass
Appeared some eyes;
Nothing'll last
If you believe in lies,
Traded dreams
To break at seams,
Lost all my tokens
For this economy
Where soft words were spoken
In lost autonomy.

Head over heels in love with the stars,
Feeling in the hills among the shootin' stars,
Stuck in the rhythm of a northbound freight
To the buffalo jump bars
In the streets and the cars,
For just a thumb to catch a ride that's late
I rode on through the gate.

Cowboy up before the sun,
Ride through ground shadow
To lope into a run;
Where do feelings go?
First sunlight on the mountain
On top of Sheep Mountain
Down to above the canyon rims.
Dove on limbs
Thought of you since I've been up
To see myself in coffee cup,
Back in time with the movement of a horse
Awake to kiss, and I love you,
Sweet smell mist, let it take its course
For my heart is two, because of you.

Wolf Teeth Mountains Rosebud Mountains on the map,
but Wolf Teeth to author's people, the Crow

A RARE FIND

RANDALL RIEMAN

It's a wonderful thing,
Though it's hard to explain,
When you meet a new friend on your way,
And you know, in no time,
There's a reason behind
The ease that your friendship's obtained;
For your spirits are one,
Though your friendship's begun
Only just a few hours ago;
Yet the things that you share
And the feelin' that's there
Is more lasting and precious than gold.

Well, your talk ran from cattle
To horses, to shoeing,
To starting these colts a new way.
And before your own eyes
The time has flown by;
Adios is the thing you now say.
But you sure hate to go,
And your feelin's, they show
On your face as you shake your friend's hand.
Still, you know that you're lucky
To have this new friend
Who shares your same love for the land,
For horses and cattle,
For life in the saddle
And nights underneath a clear sky.
A sameness in spirit that goes beyond words—
We share that, my new friend and I.

As I lift up my head
From my old canvas bed,
I thank the good Lord for His care
And for my new friend,
May we soon meet again,
For I know we have much more to share.
See, our spirits are one,
Though our friendship's begun
Only just a few hours ago.
Still, the things that we share
And the feelin' that's there
Is more lasting and precious than gold.

BULLHIDE CHAPS
AND MEMORIES

JIM SHELTON

Today I talked to Madge
      Where she tends her little store;
She's still a handsome woman
      At the age of sixty-four.
We talked of many things
      'Fore I left her at the door;
Her face still shows me strength,
      Like the bullhide chaps you wore.

She reminds, and I remember,
      Of the many years before—
The days that we were partners,
      'Fore they called me off to war.
I was only twelve,
      And now I'm thirty-four,
But I can remember our first meeting
      And the bullhide chaps you wore.

I was riding a little black—
      I called him Picador—
Just a hungry, button orphan
      Wanting work at doing chore.
You told me light a shuck,
      I needn't hunt no more,
You happened to be the foreman
      Of the rafter forty-four.

I went to herding horses;
      I'll ne'er forget, for sure,
You treated me like a hand
      And a man right to the core.

I admired your reckless daring
    And good nature there in store;
I liked your cut of brush-pop*
    In the bullhide chaps you wore.

In two years we quit the outfit
    To go it on our own,
Partners for catching wild ones
    In the peaks of the Mogollon.
We had a string of horses
    And catch-dogs—there were two;
One we called Ole Ring
    And the other one was Blue.

We gave those mossies* fits
    On the peaks of the Gavilan.*
We knew the brushy points
    Where the longhorn, ladrones* ran
Down that Bullard Canyon
    Through the boulders and the pools.
We ran down many a one
    Of those mossback, crazy fools.

Yes, sir, rawhide ropes and hobbles—
    I remember all so well—
Pack saddles and stubborn hardtails
    And a sweaty horses's smell;
The jingle of nine-star rowels*
    On a long-shank, goose-neck spur;
The slobber of wild heifers
    When we burnt the brand in fur;

Hard-oak fires, gravy brown,
    And salt-side bacon grease;
Sourdough bread and clear mountain water
    And syrup—call it lick, if you please;
Bed tarps and cowhide vests;
    Tobacco in a little rag sack;
Fry them spuds and blacktail steaks
    And boil that coffee black;

High-heel boots and stirrup taps;
    Hats better latch to the throat;
Number two steel and horse-shoe nails;
    Diamond hitches with a big pack rope;
Lead stock, the homing kind—
    I remember them all and more.
But they all remind of you, Thad,
    And the bullhide chaps you wore.

We saved our money careful,
    Bought an outfit of our own.
You met and married Madge;
    We built for her a home.
She became a welcome to us both,
    Waiting in the door,
As dependable and as dauntless
    As the bullhide chaps you wore.

We kept on catching wild ones
      And stocked our little spread.
Madge took the books and tallies
      And kept us from the red.
With work and friendship and laughter
      We built it to fair size.
Talk of three most happy people,
      I bet we took the prize.

Then the day I got the letter,
      "Your friends have chosen you,"
You stroked your grizzled mustache
      And gazed into the blue.
In Madge's eyes were tears,
      And you walked out the door;
I caught you at the corrals
      With the bullhide chaps you wore.

"I've still got ten days, Thad,"
      I told you standing by;
You raised your head quite slowly
      And looked me in the eye:
"Jim, we've caught some wild ones,"
      You told me slow and sure,
"But that don't make it easy—
      It's not the same as war.

"Spend ten days with Madge,
      And I will do the work.
These things don't bother men—
      It's the women that they hurt."
Then you stretched yourself up proud,
      And at a horse you swore,
Trying to be as tough
      As the bullhide chaps you wore.

Then came the day I left,
  When we stood to say goodbye;
The wind was sure not blowing,
  No dust was in the sky;
Madge gave way to tears,
  It was okay for her to cry;
But it's not the way of men—
  You got something in your eye.

Four years and things were better,
  The end of war in sight;
We'd fought a war like men,
  Things began to work out right.
And then I got a letter,
  It said we'd ride no more.
I thought of hands like rawhide
  And the bullhide chaps you wore.

I knew the ways of men, Thad,
  But I somehow didn't care;
I could see a weathered face
  And that thatch of graying hair.
I'd always kept the tears back,
  But I held them back no more,
For she'd sent a piece of leather
  From the bullhide chaps you wore.

When I came home to Madge,
  The ranch was not the same.
We both knew just what was missing,
  But we gave it not your name.
She showed me round the place
  In hopes I'd take it o'er,
But I couldn't fill the boots
  Nor the bullhide chaps you wore.

I gave to Madge my part;
  And I'd be running still,
But she talked me into school
  On the student G.I. bill.

Madge sold our little outfit
    And bought a little store;
The only thing she kept
    Was the bullhide chaps you wore.

She helped me with my schooling;
    I'm an educated man;
You couldn't tell by looking
    That I'd ever been a hand.
I learned the English language,
    I can speak it smart and fair;
But I can't be high-toned here,
    Have you scratching old, gray hair.

Yes, the last ten years or so
    Have really brought a change—
You never hear a puncher squall
    Nor brush poppin' on the range;
They've quit the use of rawhide,
    And the mossies are no more,
But there's two who will remember
    With the bullhide chaps you wore.

Pick a place in heaven
    That has wild ones by the score;
Pick a mountain, grassy valley;
    Open wide your cabin door,
For Madge and I will meet you
    On the cowboy's golden shore,
And we'll give back this piece of leather
    And the bullhide chaps you wore.

brush-pop brush popping against leggings and saddle gear
mossies (or mossbacks) cows so wild they seldom see a
human
Gavilan in San Francisco Mountains just across Arizona
line from Catron County, NM
ladrones (stags) wild bulls not fit to be left bulls, but
unbranded, not castrated
rowel revolving disk with sharp points at the end of a spur

MESSAGE IN THE WIND

JESSE SMITH

As you set and look from the ridge,
  To the valley of green down below,
You reach up and pull down yer lid,
  As a cool wind starts to blow.

Yer old pony's eyes are a-lookin',
  his ears workin' forward and back.
All of a sudden you feel his hide tighten,
  And a little hump come into his back.

That hoss's a readin' a message,
  That's been sent to him in the breeze.
You feel yer gut start to tighten,
  And a shakin' come into yer knees.

Ya look to the right and see nothin',
  Ya look to the left, it's the same.
Except for the birds, rabbits, and squirrels,
  And two hawks a-playin' a game.

But you know yer old hoss ain't a-lying,
  He's as good'ne as you'll ever find.
And you know that old pony's tryin'
  To warn ya 'bout somethin' in time.

Well, ya look real hard where he's lookin',
  His eyes are plum fixed in a stare,
Then ya see what he's seein',
  A cub and an old mama bear.

The trail you'd a took went between them,
  That old mama bear'd a got tough.
That old pony like as not saved yer hide,
  Or a life shortenin' scare, shor-a-nuff.

You watch 'em go 'cross the meadow,
     And ya ride on yer way once again,
And ya shor thank the Lord for the message,
     He sent to yer hoss on the wind.

I F

MARIE W. SMITH

If I hadn't become a cowboy's wife,
I'd have never seen the glow
Of night-lights on the crusted drift
Of freshly fallen snow.

I'd never have heard a barn owl cry
Outside my cabin door.
I'd never have raised Rhode Island Reds
And lost all of them but four

To a mother sow, a badger,
The owls in roosting trees,
Then to coons and rattlers
And someone else's big deep freeze.

The chicken-every-Sunday dream
Never did materialize,
But if we had had no problems,
It would be hard to realize

That there's more to raising chickens
Than picking up from the Shoshone stage,
The box of mash and fluffy chicks
When raising your own was all the rage.

If I hadn't been a cowboy's wife,
I'd have never known the grief
Of losing steers to river breaks,
Of doctoring those retrieved.

I'd never have known the coyote
Who'd visit me at four
Each day against the winter sky,
Up a Wapshili* draw.

I'd never have known the smell of sage
Right after a welcome rain,
Or known the sounds of bawling cows
From the corral at weaning time.

I'd never have known what it was like
To hush a two-year-old,
And watch a doe and this year's fawn
Behind my cabin, while the gold

Of Indian summer's final fling
Touched the meadow's ripened grass,
And blue jays screamed a warning
That summer was nigh past.

I'd never have learned to love
The joys and trials of western life,
If I'd stayed and lived Down Under,
And not become a cowboy's wife.

Wapshili winter cowcamp located about 65 air miles south
of Lewiston, Idaho, named for Wapshili Creek, which flows
into the Salmon River near where the Salmon flows in to
the Snake.

THE ROUNDUP

MARIE W. SMITH

I was a bride of just three weeks
When my husband said to me,
"I'll be gone tomorrow for about three days,
It's the roundup, d'y'see?"

I figured I knew what a roundup was,
I'd seen Gene Autry in one,
And I envisioned campfires bright,
Music, a full moon above.

"But where will we sleep?" I naively asked,
"Aw, honey, our wives don't come."
"No women at all?" I asked aghast,
The movies couldn't be *that* wrong!

"Well, a couple of 'em, Juanite and Mrs. Knight,
They cook, but that's all there'll be;
Roundup's a man's work, honey,
I'll be back in no time, you'll see."

"How'll I ever live for three long days
Without you? I could cry!"
Helpless, he said, "Wa-a-l, *may*be you can,
I'll take the pup tent and we'll tie

It up to an arm on the Reo's bed,
But I'll be gone riding hard each day."
"Oh, that's all right." (Ah, those starlit nights.)
"I won't get in your way."

His first day of riding, he'd been gone for two years,
They were ready long before dawn;
From Belleview and Hailey and Carey they came,
Association cowboys all.

I helped with the meals, I was glad I'd come,
And my heart it skipped a beat
When I saw my love returning.
I wanted to run and greet

Him, but I shyly held back
And listened to cowboys all tease,
"She's still there awaitin', Cec," they said,
"Looks like she's aimin' t' please!"

He laughed, then I blushed, and turned
To help with the spuds and the meat.
He winked and grabbed and loaded a plate;
My heart flopped and I ached to greet.

We'd rigged up the tent and just crawled thru the
    flap
And, bone tired, he doffed hat and boots,
And there he was, asleep in a minute
Like he didn't give two hoots

For the bride at his side. I snuggled and slept.
All of a sudden, horses were stomping around.
I shook him, "Quick, we've overslept!"
"Damn!" was his only sound.

And then we heard the voices
Of brothers a little away,
"Ain't it disgustin'," I heard Lowell drawl,
"To sleep this long in the day?"

"It surely is," Sherm answered him,
"What do you think we oughta do?"
"Why, cut it down on 'em," said Lowell with a laugh,
"That'll teach 'em not to snooze."

Horrified I turned to Cec,
"They're gonna cut down the tent!"
"Naw, they wouldn't do that," he said
As he pulled on his high-crowned hat.

I rolled to grab clothes, and he his boots,
But neither was fast enough,
The tent tumbled down about us,
And then it was really tough.

We must have looked like two cats in a sack,
As we struggled to find clothes and dress.
"I should have stayed home," I thought to myself,
"Gosh, what a terrible mess!"

When we'd finally dressed, Cec, like a gentleman,
    said,
"O.K., dear, ladies first."
I was glad that he was so polite,
With little air my lungs felt to burst.

I found my direction and crawled right out
Through the flap, only to view
Not only two pair of legs clad in chaps and boots,
There must have been twenty-two.

I felt then that I should make
Some excuse for being late.
The only one that came to mind
Was, "Cec couldn't find his hat."

Then I followed the bow in old Frank Knight's legs
As he teased with a crusty chuckle,
"Y' mean to say he took off his *hat* to sleep?
How about his belt buckle?"

The cowboys roared, Cec laughed with them,
And, O.K., my lesson I learned,
That a roundup's no place for a greenhorn bride,
You know—I've never returned.

OUR RANGE

ERIC SPRADO

The beauty, the beauty, my pen can't quite share,
Tho' I'll do my best to put you there.

One of those magic evenings in Butte Valley,
Riding south, the sun on my right,
Perched on top of the Rubies,*
A big orange ball of fire about to
Roll off the other side and take away
What little heat it had shared with me that day,
The moon, its twin on my left,
Was balanced on Palomino Ridge,
Somehow announcing to the purple hills below
That it was ready to take the night shift.

I was heading for the house, riding old "Punch."
We'd been to check the north end well.
It was cold, God, it was cold—
Probably twenty degrees below—
The only noise made by Punch's hooves
As they crunched through frozen snow.

Breath freezing to my beard, feet light in the stirrups,
Wiggling my toes to see if they were still there.
Punch's head came up and he stopped short.
There was magic in the air.

Ten yards away I saw old "Three Toes"—
Daddy of all the coyotes that had ever
Eaten one of my lambs.
He'd lost three toes off his right front foot
In one of my traps back in '78.
Just a pup then, but it's a tough old world,
And he went to school that day.

We'd been at war ever since,
With a strange mixture of love and hate.
I'd sworn to put a hole in him
For every lamb he ate.

Time stood still. We stared at each other.
Somehow, in those seconds I came to understand
How he and I, both renegades,
Belong to the very same land.

You and all the other wolves
Who make a living on this place
Doing what you were put here to do,
Without shame or disgrace.

Eat or die seven days a week.
A day's work for a day's pay.
You don't even have to bow
To the BLM or the FHA.

Again and again that thought:
Who belongs on this range?
Humans, who are always wanting more,
Or coyotes, who never change?

All of these thoughts flew through my head
As in those few seconds we stared.
We both belong here, you and I,
In this special place we share.

Yours by birthright; it's your home
Sure as you stare at the moon and howl.
Mine by a strangely human rite;
I got it by grab root and growl.

So on this magic evening
With the sun and moon as my witness,
I'll share with you.

Tomorrow our war we'll re-declare,
But with an attitude that's changed.
We'll still be enemies until the death,
But we both belong on this,
      Our range.

Rubies Ruby Mountain Range in northeastern Nevada

WAIT 'TIL YOU BECOME A MAN

ERIC SPRADO

I remember seeing men
Who lost their farms in the thirties—
Deep lines and haunted looks
Carved into those faces.

Why do those men look angry and sad?
I asked as a little boy.
You're too young to understand, son;
Wait 'til you're a man.

I grew up and forgot that look.
Good times were here to stay.
Drifting around, having fun,
Still, putting money away.

Finally, my dream come true.
A ranch of my own.

In harsh sagebrush country,
Hot in the summer, cold in the winter,
A country that makes you feel big and small,
Covered with alkali dust, I could
Break off a piece of sagebrush and say,
        "I love you."

Herding cows in a blizzard, I could
Lay back my head and
        Laugh like a madman.

Now it's gone.
The deep, deep lines and haunted look
I think I understand.
Maybe I've become a man.

BEDROLL

RED STEAGALL

There's a hole in the wagonsheet big as my head
Where coosie run under a tree.
Last week it rained and poured right in that hole;
Probably nobody noticed but me.

'Cause that was the mornin' I jingled the horses.
It rained and my bed was just fine.
But it was the first one to go in the wagon
And the rest of 'em stacked up on mine.

Last winter we put a new floor in that wagon,
We planked it with tongue and groove oak.
She's tight as a drum and won't leak a drop.
So the bed on the bottom got soaked.

Now canvas is good about turnin' the dew
As long as it's stretched the right way.
But I guess something happens, it sorta breaks down
Sittin' in water all day.

Your bed's usually warm and a nice place to be,
A cowpuncher's private domain.
But it's colder'n hell in a bedroll that's wet;
You're better off out in the rain.

So I put on my slicker and sat by the fire,
Burned all the dry wood in the stack.
The fire made me drowsy—once I dozed off
And woke up in the mud, on my back.

Just before sunup I crawled in that bed,
Couldn't sleep 'cause my feet were so numb.
Then coosie was cussin' I burned all his wood,
So I got up and gathered him some.

Now I ain't one to argue and create a fuss
And I don't get my head in a fog.
But it's taken a week for me to get her dried out,
And last night I slept like a log.

This mornin' it's thunderin' and carryin' on.
It's already startin' to rain.
And I know for a fact coosie ain't fixed that hole
And I ain't goin' through that again.

Everyone's saddled and ready to ride
Except me, and I'll be here awhile.
I wanta make sure that when they load up the wagon
My bed's on the top of the pile.

THE WEATHER

RED STEAGALL

There's something about a cool October mornin'
That suits my disposition just right.
The sky is as clear as a crystal today
And as the sun slowly creeps into sight,

My old pony's step is a little bit lighter;
Must be the crisp autumn air.
Cold weather's comin', no doubt about that,
He's growed a half inch of long hair.

I just saw some geese headin' south for the winter.
That shore is a beautiful sight.
Something inside of me stirs at the sound
Of Canadian honkers in flight.

The pronghorn are startin' to gather in bunches—
A sign winter's well on her way.
The mesquite trees have put on a good crop of beans.
Be a tough one the old timers say.

The boys and I cleared eighty acres of pasture.
We laid in 'bout 10 cord of wood.
Burnin' mesquite is the cowboy's perfume,
Makes that musty old cabin smell good.

Me and the missus snuggle up to the fire.
We read a book when the snow gets too deep.
Course I'm gettin' to where I only get through two
    pages
'Fore my old mind drifts off to sleep.

Lately I've noticed some pain in my joints,
Gets worse as the weather gets cold.
The Doc says I need to go someplace that's warm,
But shoot, it's just age taking hold.

My neighbor got him a place down in Scottsdale;
He leaves here before the first snow.
But there ain't no way in hell I could go to the
    desert,
Wouldn't last maybe three days or so.

'Cause I'd get to missin' my chores in the winter—
I get up every morning at five.
And I'd worry that if I wasn't right here to feed 'em,
There's a chance that my cows won't survive.

I'm right partial to cows, I'm there when they're
    calvin'.
The missus gives each one a name.
When they're older we cull 'em and thin out the
    dinks,
But when they're babies they all look the same.

Most people seem to like springtime the best,
When everything's fresh, clean and clear.
But fall seems to say, hey, it's time to slow down;
You've worked hard enough for one year.

I do look forward to April—there's one special place
Where I planted bluebonnets last year.
I hope they come up, they're my favorite flower.
That's one reason I like it out here.

Listen to me, I'm just ramblin' around.
Wouldn't change things if I had the chance.
The weather don't matter, I ain't goin' nowhere.
There's no place I'd trade for this ranch.

HAILSTORM

COLEN H. SWEETEN, JR.

I remember the deafening roar,
The wavering fields of wheat,
The huddled family—
A sudden chilling of the July heat,
And fear in my father's eyes—
My father who kicked badgers
And laughed at broncos!
Mother quietly put her arm around him
As if she feared he might rush,
Bare-fisted, to battle the icy pellets.

I remember my father's eyes, filled
With tears as big as toadstools.
Icy tears which just hung there.
There was too much pride to fall,
And too much hurt to retreat.
And then our harvest was over.
Our valley was still, oh, so still.

Soon the hurt was healing.
There was no bitterness.
There was no blame.
I knew my parents still trusted God.

Now, in the quiet of my own silent hailstorms,
When I alone am aware of the roar,
I feel a strength from that old scar,
And find courage born of faith,
Not of understanding.

THE BUCKING HORSE MOON

PAUL ZARZYSKI

A kiss for luck, then we'd let 'er buck—
I'd spur electric on adrenaline and lust.
She'd figure-8 those barrels
on her Crimson Missile sorrel—
we'd make the night air swirl with hair and dust.

At some sagebrushed wayside, 3 A.M.,
we'd water, grain, and ground-tie Missile,
zip our sleeping bags together,
make love in any weather,
amid the cactus, rattlers, and thistle.

Seems the moon was always full for us—
its high-diving shadow kicking hard.
We'd play kid games on the big night sky;
she'd say, "That bronco's Blue-Tail Fly,
and ain't that ol' J.T. spurrin' off its stars?"

We knew sweet youth's no easy keeper.
It's spent like winnings, all too soon.
So we'd revel every minute
in the music of our Buick
running smooth—two rodeoin' lovers
cruising to another—
beneath Montana's blue roan
bucking horse moon.

The Augusta perf* at 2—we'd place again,
then sneak off to our secret Dearborn River spot.
We'd take some chips and beer and cheese,
skinny-dip, dry off in the breeze,
build a fire, fry the trout we caught.

Down moonlit gravel back to blacktop,
she'd laugh and kill those beams for fun.
That old wagon road was ours to own.
Thirty shows since I'd been thrown
and eighty-seven barrels since she'd tipped one.

We knew that youth won't keep for rainy days;
It burns and turns to ash too soon.
So we'd revel every minute
in the music of our Buick
running smooth, two rodeoin' lovers
cruising to another—
beneath Montana's blue roan
bucking horse moon.

perf abbreviation for performance

In memory of Joe Lear

ALL THIS WAY FOR
THE SHORT RIDE

PAUL ZARZYSKI

After grand entry cavalcade of flags,
Star Spangled Banner, stagecoach figure 8's
in a jangle of singletrees,* after trick riders
sequined in tights, clowns in loud getups,
queens sashed pink or chartreuse
in silk—after the fanfare—the domed
rodeo arena goes lights-out
black: stark silent
prayer for a cowboy crushed by a ton
of crossbred Brahma.

                  What went wrong—
too much heart behind a high kick,
both horns hooking earth, the bull vaulting
a half-somersault to its back—
each witness recounts with the same
gruesome note: the wife
stunned in a bleacher seat
and pregnant with their fourth. In this dark
behind the chutes, I strain to picture,
through the melee of win with loss,
details of a classic ride—body curled
fetal to the riggin', knees up,
every spur stroke in perfect sync,
chin tucked snug. In this dark,
I rub the thick neck of my bronc, his pulse
rampant in this sudden night
and lull. I know the instant
that bull's flanks tipped beyond

return, how the child inside
fought with his mother for air
and hope, his heart with hers
pumping in pandemonium—in shock,
how she maundered in the arena
to gather her husband's bullrope and hat, bells
clanking to the murmur of crowd
and siren's mewl.

           The child learned early
through pain the amnion could not protect him from,
through capillaries of the placenta, the sheer
peril of living with a passion
that shatters all at once
from infinitesimal fractures
in time. It's impossible,
when dust settling to the backs of large animals
makes a racket you can't think in,
impossible to conceive that pure fear,
whether measured in degrees of cold
or heat, can both freeze
and incinerate so much
in mere seconds. When I nod
and they throw this gate open to the same
gravity, the same 8 ticks
of the clock, number 244 and I
will blow for better or worse
from this chute—flesh and destiny up
for grabs, a bride's bouquet
pitched blind.

singletree same as whiffletree—the swinging bar to which
the traces of a harness are fastened and by which a stage-
coach is drawn

For Larry, Curt, Joel, Jim and Bugs

THE HEAVYWEIGHT CHAMPION
PIE-EATIN' COWBOY
OF THE WEST

PAUL ZARZYSKI

I just ate 50 pies—started off with coconut
macaroon, wedged my way through bar angel
chocolate, Marlborough, black walnut and sour cream
raisin to confetti-crusted crab apple—
still got room for dessert
and they can stick their J-E-L-L-O
where the cowpie don't shine, 'cause, Sugar Plum,
I don't eat nothing made from horses' hooves!

So make it something "pie," something light
and fancy, like huckleberry fluffy chiffon, go
extra heavy on the hucks and fluff—beaten
egg whites folded in *just* so. Or let's shoot
for something in plaid, red and tan lattice-
topped raspberry, honeyed crust
flaky and blistered to a luster, wild
fruit oozing with a scoop of hard vanilla!

Or maybe I'll strap on a feedbag of something
a smidgen more timid: quivering
custard with its nutmeg-freckled fill
nervous in the shell. Come to think of it now,
blue ribbon mincemeat sounds a lot
more my cut: neck of venison, beef suet,
raisins, apples, citrus peel, currants—
all laced, Grammy-fashion, in blackstrap molasses!

No. Truth is, I'm craving shoofly or spiced rhubarb,
or sure hard to match peachy praline,
cinnamon winesap apple á la mode, walnut
crumb or chocolate pecan. OR,
whitecapped high above its fluted deep-dish crust,
a lemon angel meringue—not to mention
mandarin apricot, black bottom, banana cream,
burgundy berry or Bavarian nectarine ambrosia!

And how could you out-gun the Turkeyday
old reliables: sweet potato, its cousin
pumpkin, its sidekicks Dutch apple and cranberry
ice cream nut. Ah, harvest moon, that autumn
gourmet cheese supreme, or Jack Frost squash, or . . .
"my favorite," you ask? That's a tough one.
Just surprise me with something new, Sweetie
Pie—like tangerine boomerang gooseberry!

BIOGRAPHIES

DARRELL ARNOLD • Colorado Springs, Colorado

Darrell Arnold was born and raised in the small ranching community of La Veta, Colorado, in the south-central portion of the state. Though he wasn't raised on a ranch, his family owned livestock, including cattle, hogs, sheep, and horses. He spent many hours horseback on fishing and hunting trips in the nearby mountains, and cowboyed, occasionally, for local ranchers. Arnold has a B.S. degree in wildlife biology from Colorado State University. In the early eighties he was a hunting guide and outfitter before turning full time to journalism. In 1985 he became associate editor at *Western Horseman* magazine, where he is also poetry editor, and he travels the West doing photographic features about cowboys, ranchers, and westerners.

FIN BAYLES • Blanding, Utah

Fin was plunged into ranching life right from the start and spent his youth doing chores and dispatching rattlesnakes. After serving in the Korean War, he graduated from college, taught in high school off and on, and wended his way back to the family ranch, where he lives now. He has a fancy little bunch of hybrid cattle, does a little farming, and sells pitrun gravel to the contractors. He and his wife, Jill, enjoy their seven children and the grandkids.

ED BROWN • Merced, California

Ed has worked on cow outfits for twenty years, the last twelve in California. Recalling the recitation of classic poems in cowcamps when he was young and the renewed popular interest in cowboy poetry sparked Ed to write some of his own. "When I tell my stories to people, I'm a liar; but if they rhyme, I'm a poet."

BOB CHRISTENSEN • Syracuse, Utah

Bob presently lives on part of the place his grandfather homesteaded. He has been associated with the ranching industry for twenty-eight years as a representative of Pillsbury's Best Feeds, calling on ranches in Utah, Idaho, Wyoming, Nevada, and Montana. He has been featured at the Elko gathering the past few years and has published two books of humorous cowboy poetry.

JOHN DOFFLEMEYER • Lemon Cove, California

John runs a cow and calf operation in the foothills of the Sierra Nevada, below Sequoia National Park, as did four generations before him. Poetry has been a therapeutic exercise since the age of thirteen; today it is an enjoyable habit, almost a compulsion. His subject matter deals primarily with the feelings and meanings acquired in his environment—Mother Nature. His high regard for the old values of friendship and community often come into conflict with urban growth and development in his poetry. He hopes to evoke an emotional response from the reader, perhaps even some thought.

LEON FLICK • Plush, Oregon

Leon lives in a small town of about fifty people in the high desert country of eastern Oregon. He has spent most of his life working on cattle ranches in Lake and Harney counties and has also spent a little time in California and northeastern Oregon. He tends to enjoy working on cow-calf outfits more than yearling operations.

KAY KELLEY • Santa Fe, New Mexico

Kay was a born rider and cowgirl; she has that look that guarantees she's at home horseback. She first came into contact with cowboy poetry by way of her first husband's poetry writings about the experiences of a horse trainer and cowboy in the Southwest. After his death, Kay began writing her own poetry. Her favorite topics are the action of work, the personalities of horses, and the quirks of ranching life. She is married to Brian Kelley, who was born and raised on a family ranch in Val Verde County, Texas.

MIKE LOGAN • Helena, Montana

Raised in Coffeyville, Kansas, Mike moved to Montana twenty years ago. Though he comes from a ranching background, he has spent his professional life as a ranch and wildlife photographer and a teacher. For years he has been writing poems about ranch life and the old-time cattle industry. He has made many friends at ranches all over the state, where he is often asked to hold forth his poems in his low, booming voice.

GARY McMAHAN • Bellvue, Colorado

Gary was raised with horses and cows. His father ran a cattle trucking business in Greeley, where Gary grew up straddling between school friends who he describes as cowboys and surfers. His adult life has been spent trying to make it in both the entertainment and horse businesses. Gary is most famous for having the slipperiest yodel in the West and for writing the cowboy classic "The Double Diamond." He makes ends meet by running the Double Diamond riding stables in the Rocky Mountains above Fort Collins. He is particularly interested in how cowboys are tested by life and how they respond.

ROD McQUEARY • Ruby Valley, Nevada

Rod was born and raised in Ruby Valley, Nevada. He lives and runs cattle on his family's ranch. He picks a little guitar. His long humorous poems are especially popular with audiences. He is a Vietnam veteran. Rod is married, and he and Monica have three children.

WALLACE McRAE • Forsyth, Montana

The McRae family is in the fifth generation ranching on Rosebud Creek, just south of Colstrip, Montana. Wallace's grandfather came from Scotland to southeastern Montana in 1882. During the infamous winter of 1886-87, John B. McRae watched his sheep die, one by one, until when spring finally came he had only the pelts, which he sold in order to purchase the 160 acres that started the McRae Ranch. Ever since, the McRaes have fought to survive and carve out a life in the red scoria hills of eastern Montana. The latest threat has been the industrialization of the area due to coal strip mines. McRae uses his poetry to give light to a message of cultural preservation. McRae is best known for his classic poem "Reincarnation," which is recited all over cattle country. Although "Reincarnation" is a humorous poem, he is recognized also for his serious and insightful writing. He has had three books of poetry published and is a popular university lecturer and performer.

WADDIE MITCHELL • Lee-Jiggs, Nevada
If the American public knows of a cowboy poet, it is likely to be Waddie Mitchell, who has made several appearances on "The Tonight Show." He is best known for his recitations of the classic folk poems from the cowboy tradition and his inimitable handlebar mustache. Waddie grew up on his father's ranch and vowed someday he would own his own. After working as a buckaroo on several large spreads, he settled down, married, had five kids, and worked his way up to managing ranches. He is currently managing the Elko Ranch near Jiggs, Nevada. He knows that his dream of owning his own ranch will never happen on cowboy wages, so he spends a lot of his time promoting cowboy in appearances around the country.

BARNEY NELSON • Alpine, Texas
Barney lives with her husband, Joel, and their daughter, Carla, at Willow Springs Camp on the 06 Ranch. Barney is completing a graduate degree in English, where she is working with the literature of Shakespeare and his lessons about horsemanship. She organizes the Texas Cowboy Poetry Gathering and has written and photographed extensively on cowboy life. She has also edited a book on Texas cowboy poetry, but says everything truly worthwhile was done horseback.

JOEL NELSON • Alpine, Texas
Joel is a camp man on the famous 06 Ranch near Alpine, one of the few ranches that still pulls the wagon out for roundups. A Vietnam vet, Joel describes his own poetry as "reflecting the appreciation I have for the modern cowboy and his absolute refusal to turn loose of what was good from the past."

ROD NELSON • Bismark, North Dakota
Rod lives on a small ranch in southwestern North Dakota with his wife, Teri, and children, Annika and Lafe. He has ranched all his life and also trains horses and participates in rodeos whenever he can. He is the local brand inspector and enjoys performing his poetry across the country.

HOWARD NORSKOG • St. Anthony, Idaho
Howard was raised around Cody, Wyoming, close to the famous Wild Bill Cody ranch. As a young man, Howard rode the mountains of Wyoming that he says inspired him to begin writing poems in 1948. His first

inspiration was Robert Service, though his poems now center on the wild beauty of open land and the relationship of man and horse to the land.

GWEN PETERSEN • Big Timber, Montana

Gwen started life in Illinois and spent summers on her grandparents' farm, where she developed a yen for country life. She moved to Montana after high school and later graduated from the University of Puget Sound with a degree in occupational therapy. She lives on a small ranch with her husband and an assortment of cows, pigs, sheep, horses, chickens, cats, dogs, geese and several uninvited varmints. For three years Gwen has been project director for the Montana Cowboy Poetry Gathering. She made an appearance on the "Tonight Show." She is a banquet speaker-humorist, writes a syndicated column, is a published author with six books to her credit and is presently working on three more book projects.

VESS QUINLAN • Alamosa, Colorado

Vess used laser technology to design a vastly more efficient irrigation system for the San Luis Valley Ranch, which he and some partners owned. After withdrawing from the longtime ranch partnership in 1985, the entire Quinlan family—Vess, Arla, and three grown children—moved to Tucson, Arizona. Vess enrolled in poetry classes at Pima College and creative writing classes at the University of Arizona. He was dismayed to find a strong bias against the kind of traditional rhyming poems he liked to write. Several instructors and workshop leaders suggested he experiment with the more modern free-verse form while keeping his subjects and ranch perspective, and he has tried to do so. When the old partners defaulted on several loans, an old friend and new partner helped regain the land. The family is starting over broke but glad to be home.

BUCK RAMSEY • Amarillo, Texas

Buck spent his cowboy days snappin' out broncs and punchin' cattle on the big ranches along the Canadian River in the Panhandle of Texas. Some years ago he got stove up and put in a wheel chair by a horse bigger than he was and some ranch tack that tore all to pieces. He still keeps his hand in the game, though, as hoodlum helper to the cookie, giving guff from the opry seats, plucking and singing the old songs, and braiding tack. And maybe, with more time on his hands, he pays more attention now.

GENE RANDELS • Greeley, Colorado

Born in a sod house and raised during the Great Depression, Gene hoboed across the country taking day work as a cowboy and any job he could find. He even did a stint as a professional boxer. But he always gravitated back to horses and cows. After being cowboss on a couple of Wyoming ranches, he bought his own place. The last few years he worked at a feedlot in Greeley. Gene passed away August 21, 1989, to once again find the Black Wolf and ride the Dry Willow and Arikaree.

HENRY REAL BIRD • Garryowen, Montana
Hank was born into an influential Crow Indian family. His writing explores the intersections between the cowboy's life of rodeo, cattle markets, and modern technology and the ancient stories of the Crow mythology and spirituality of man and the environment. He holds a degree from Montana State University and has written songs, poetry and children's books.

RANDALL J. RIEMAN • Lovelock, Nevada
Randy is in his mid-thirties and, although he currently lives in Nevada, he considers Montana his home. Randy was not born into ranching but has chosen to make his living cowboying. For the past ten years he has lived in Montana, working on various ranches, for grazing associations, doing day work, and riding a few colts. He has collected cowboy songs and poetry for years.

ERIC SPRADO • Junction City, Oregon
As the son of a German father and Russian mother who immigrated to the United States just before World War II, Eric has a proud feeling about the opportunity to do what he wants to do. At one time he owned a ranch a long way from anywhere between Wells and Ely, Nevada, but due to harsh economics the ranch was lost. He is a big bearded man who makes his living shoeing horses. Eric has been a fiddle player and singer all his life and is doing something with his music he always wanted to do—sharing it with special-ed kids in the local schools.

JIM SHELTON • Glenwood, New Mexico
Jim was born to a cow outfit in 1925. He worked for his dad until he was twelve, when he went to work on other outfits. He did time in the armed forces and graduated from Western New Mexico University at twenty-four. Jim has written poems and songs right through it all and put icing on the cake with a few novels. He's turned a hand to drilling wells, windmilling, breaking horses, and predator control, as well as writing. But through his poems you'll hear the heart of a cowboy ringing true.

JESSE SMITH • Springville, California
Jesse grew up in a little mountain town of Glenville, California, on the west slope of the Sierras. He worked on local ranches until age fifteen, then decided to quit school and go to work full time packing; he just wanted to make a living horseback. He worked on outfits all around the San Joaquin Valley until he went into the service in 1959, where he spent thirty-one months with the 82nd Airborne Division. After his discharge he worked a few months in Texas, then worked his way up to Alaska, but returned to California 1963. He's settled now, with a wife and two daughters and even one grandson. He has a handful of cows and some pretty fair horses. Jesse works full time for Merritt Ranches, which runs about 400 head of mother cows.

MARIE W. SMITH • Somers, Montana

Born in 1927 in west Australia, Marie emigrated to the U.S. in 1952 and married Cecil Smith, an Idaho cowboy and western artist. Her ranching experiences have been on the Bar Bell ranches at Carey and Lewiston, Idaho, and on the Clearview Ranch near Somers. She is the mother of eleven and has ten grandchildren. She studies creative writing at the community college in Kalispell and is putting together a second volume of her cowboy poetry (her first volume was published in 1988). Marie also writes other forms of poetry, children's stories, and is compiling a poetic anthology of her childhood, an autobiography, and her late husband's biography.

RED STEAGALL • Azle, Texas

Red's career in entertainment has covered a period of twenty years and has spanned the globe from Australia to the Middle East, including years promoting rodeo and the cowboy way of life. As a native Texan, Red enjoyed a career in agricultural chemistry after graduating from West Texas State University with a degree in animal science and agronomy. He then spent eight years as a music-industry executive in Hollywood, and has spent the last twelve years as a recording artist, songwriter, and television and motion picture personality. He currently offices outside of Forth Worth, Texas, where, in addition to his entertainment activities, he is involved in the production of motion pictures and television shows.

COLEN H. SWEETEN, JR. • Malad, Idaho

Colen has spent most of his life in the Curley Valley in southern Idaho. Some of his earliest memories are of being awakened before sunup by the thunder of horses' hooves as his father brought thirty or forty of their 150 head down from the mountains on a dead run. Colen has been involved in livestock and grain operations; he served as county clerk for twenty-one years and also served in state government. He sees cowboy poetry as a form of history, since much of it is based on actual experience. His poems and articles have been published in about thirty papers and magazines, ranging from the hometown weekly to *Reader's Digest*. He is retired now and has time to spend with his five children and thirteen grandchildren. Colen has participated in all the Elko gatherings.

PAUL ZARZYSKI • Augusta, Montana

Paul is a rodeo poet. Living in Montana for the past sixteen years, his life has been a passion of poetry and rodeo. He studied at the University of Montana with Richard Hugo, where he learned it might be possible to capture the intensity of rodeo with words. Paul also learned new forms of poetry and has become a major proponent of free verse as an option in the cowboy poetry tradition. He has published three books of poems, the most recent a collaboration with photographer Barbara Van Cleve.